Jesus Calling®

52-WEEK BIBLE STUDY

Experience the Presence of God

BASED ON THE BOOK BY

SARAH YOUNG

with KAREN LEE-THORP *and* KRIS BEARSS

Jesus Calling 52-Week Bible Study

Published by HarperChristian Resources, 3950 Sparks Drive SE, Suite 101, Grand Rapids, MI 49546, USA. HarperChristian Resources is a registered trademark of HarperCollins Christian Publishing, Inc.

Requests for information should be addressed to customercare@harpercollins.com.

ISBN 978-0-310-17975-7 (softcover)
ISBN 978-0-310-17976-4 (ebook)

HarperChristian Resources titles may be purchased in bulk for church, business, fundraising, or ministry use. For information, please e-mail ResourceSpecialist@ChurchSource.com.

HarperCollins Publishers, Macken House, 39/40 Mayor Street Upper, Dublin 1, D01 C9W8, Ireland (https://www.harpercollins.com).

Cover Design: Jamie DeBruyn
Interior Design: Rob Williams, InsideOut Design

First Printing October 2025 / Printed in Canada

CONTENTS

INTRODUCTION

From Genesis to Revelation, the Bible is filled with examples of God's desire to mold you into the image of Christ, reminding you that in Jesus you are loved, you are worthy, and you are made new. However, becoming Christlike doesn't happen without challenges. In fact, God's Word includes many stories of men and women who faced hardships despite their faith, including:

- **King David**, whose story reveals that even those who are faithful to God can fall away from Him. When this happens, his shout of repentance and cry for God to "create in me a clean heart" (Psalm 51:10 ESV) should be your own.
- **Elijah**, who even after mighty victories was overwhelmed by fear and depression and fell into despair. His story reveals that God will meet you where you are in your need and give you spiritual and physical renewal (see 1 Kings 19).
- **Mary**, the mother of Jesus, who faced being ostracized for being found pregnant outside of wedlock. Her story reveals the importance of surrendering your plans—and yourself—into God's hands (see Luke 1:26-38).
- **Peter**, who in a moment of crisis denied knowing Jesus three times. He went from fear to faith (see Luke 22:54-62; Acts 2:14-42), reminding you that you can fully trust and surrender to God's transforming work.
- **Paul**, a persecutor of Christians who met the risen Jesus on the road to Damascus and was radically changed by God's power (see Acts 9:1-19). He became one of the most steadfast and passionate messengers of the gospel, which demonstrates the renewal you can also find in Christ.

What these characters (and others) faced reveals the truth of Jesus' statement that "in this world you will have trouble" (John 16:33). There will be trials and times when you are tested in your faith. Yet, as these stories also show, redemption is possible. Through God's faithfulness, these individuals were renewed and restored. In the same way, God's power is sufficient to meet you where you are and transform you into the image of His Son.

The Bible reveals time and time again that this change comes not from willpower but through God's Word and the work of the Holy Spirit. When you spend time in Scripture, you allow the Spirit to renew your mind (see Romans 12:2). Paul sums it up beautifully in Colossians 3:9–10: "You have taken off your old self with its practices and have put on the new self, which is being renewed in the image of its Creator."

Goal of This Study

This 52-week study is designed to help you meditate on the words of Scripture and hear those words not just as something said to people long ago but also as something God is saying to you in the here and now. Each of the weekly studies has been created to center around a key reading from *Jesus Calling* by Sarah Young. The goal is to help your *heart* hear and respond to what your *mind* is reading—to encounter the living God as He speaks to you through the Bible. As the writer to the Hebrews has written:

> In the past God spoke to our ancestors through the prophets at many times and in various ways, but in these last days he has spoken to us by his Son, whom he appointed heir of all things, and through whom also he made the universe. The Son is the radiance of God's glory and the exact representation of his being, sustaining all things by his powerful word (1:1–3).

God has spoken through the lives of believers in both the Old and New Testaments—and particularly through Christ. The New Testament gives you the chance to walk with Jesus, see what He does, and hear Him speak into the confusing situations in which you find yourself. The Old Testament tells the story of how God prepared a people to be the family of Jesus. In the experiences of those men and women, you find your own life mirrored.

The Flow of Each Week

This study offers you the chance to lay down your cares, enter God's Presence, and hear Him speak through His Word. Each weekly study contains the following elements:

- **Discover:** This brief opener sets the tone for the material you will be studying, highlighting an introductory thought or an idea about the theme of that week. This opener is followed by two reflection questions that will help you start thinking about the content of the lesson.

- **Dwell:** Next, you will explore a key passage from God's Word connected to the topic for the week. The two reflective questions that follow will help you gain further insight into the passage.

- **Experience:** Here you will find a reading from *Jesus Calling*, along with two questions for reflection. This is your chance to review the biblical principles found within the *Jesus Calling* devotions. **(Note that direct quotes from *Jesus Calling* that appear elsewhere in this study guide appear in gold type.)**

- **Apply:** Finally, you will find seven days' worth of suggested Scripture passages and questions that correspond to that week's theme. This application will give you time *each day* to dwell in God's Word and in His Presence.

God desires you to draw closer to Him! He longs to make you more like Jesus each day so you can glorify Him in all you do. As Paul states, "[Be] confident of this very thing, that He who has begun a good work in you will complete it until the day of Jesus Christ" (Philippians 1:6 NKJV). As you spend time in God's Word each day and continue to abide in His Presence, you will find that He will do an amazing and incredible work within you!

Week 1

SPENDING TIME IN GOD'S PRESENCE

DISCOVER

God is with you right now. Do you believe that? He longs for times of stillness with you where you can learn to know Him.

Perhaps you've never thought of it this way, but He personally *invites* you to pause, listen, and take time with Him in meaningful ways each day. "Come to me," He says (Matthew 11:28). "Draw near" (James 4:8 NKJV). "Abide in me" (John 15:5 NKJV). As you take these words to heart, you'll grow increasingly aware of both His Presence and His Love for you.

In this week's study, you will learn the invaluable practice of spending time in God's Presence by reading and prayerfully interacting with Scripture. This is more than just developing a habit. Rather, it's *a way of life* that produces peace, clarity, and a deeper relationship with Him through the guidance of the Holy Spirit.

1. *What is it like for you to experience God's Presence? How strongly do you believe God wants you to experience His Presence? What hesitations, if any, do you have?*

2. *What in particular draws you to this exploration of God's Presence?*

Experience

COME TO ME with a teachable spirit, eager to be changed. A close walk with Me is a life of continual newness. Do not cling to old ways as you step into a new year. Instead, seek My Face with an open mind, knowing that your journey with Me involves being *transformed by the renewing of your mind.* As you focus your thoughts on Me, be aware that I am fully attentive to you. I see you with a steady eye because my attention span is infinite. I know and understand you completely; My thoughts embrace you in everlasting Love. *I also know the plans I have for you: plans to prosper you and not to harm you, plans to give you hope and a future.* Give yourself fully to this adventure of increasing attentiveness to My Presence.

— From *Jesus Calling*, January 1

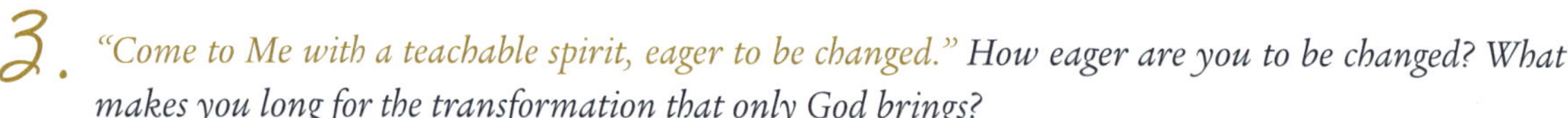

3. *"Come to Me with a teachable spirit, eager to be changed." How eager are you to be changed? What makes you long for the transformation that only God brings?*

4. *"Be aware that I am fully attentive to you." God is fully attentive to His children. Do you want that attention, or do you find the idea a bit scary? Explain your response.*

Dwell

Read Luke 10:38–42 and think about the idea of committing yourself "fully to this adventure of increasing attentiveness to [God's] Presence." Note in this story that Jesus wasn't just a guest of Martha and Mary; He was a close friend who brought peace and fellowship to their lives. Martha welcomed Him into their home, which was a sacred act of hospitality in that culture, but she missed out on the opportunity to truly experience His Presence. Meanwhile, her younger sister, Mary, sat at Jesus' feet, fully focusing in that moment on being present with Him.

5. *When you read this passage, did you see yourself reflected more in Mary or in Martha—or were you reflected equally in both? Explain your thoughts.*

6. *How did Mary demonstrate she was seeking God's Face with an open mind? What was she demonstrating by sitting at the feet of Jesus—the position of a disciple?*

7. *What was Martha's complaint to Jesus? How did Jesus demonstrate that He knew Martha and understood her well—but wanted her to reevaluate her priorities?*

8. *What might the Holy Spirit be impressing on your heart through this passage? What is He saying to you about the need to spend time in God's Presence?*

Apply

The focus of this week's readings is on spending time in God's Presence. For each of the following days this week, read the passage that is provided slowly, pausing to think about what is being said. Remember, this is an opportunity to meet with Jesus!

Day 1

Read Joshua 1:5–9. *Reread it aloud and put yourself into the scene. God has just given Joshua a new and difficult task. How do you respond as you hear God's words to him? How teachable are you in this moment? Write down whatever seems important for you to remember.*

Day 2

Read Isaiah 30:21. *Why do you think the "voice" is behind the one who yearns to do God's will? How will hearing this voice affect what you do?*

Day 3

Read Isaiah 30:22. *How do idols get in the way of experiencing God's Presence? What idols in your life might you need to throw away?*

Day 4

Read Psalm 25:4–5 several times. *What does being teachable have to do with experiencing God's Presence? What would it take for you to place your hope in the Lord "all day long"?*

Day 5

Read Isaiah 50:4–9. *How do you deal with people who condemn you—or even a voice you hear in your head? How could taking this servant's posture help you with those condemning voices?*

Day 6

Read Psalm 31:19–20. *What do you think it means to be hidden in God's Presence? What are some of the benefits that those who choose to be hidden in God receive?*

Day 7

Read Psalm 31:19–20 again. *What does this passage move you to say to God?*

Week 2
RUNNING TOWARD GOD

Discover

Let's admit it: Life's difficulties will sometimes trigger our fear instead of our faith. This seems especially true when we have sinned in some way. As much as we yearn deep down for the comfort of God's Presence, it can be tempting to make a choice other than to trust in Him. We are prone to run *from* the Lord in such situations instead of *to* Him.

Nevertheless, God loves us! He loves us so much that He sent His Son to die for us. As Paul wrote, "God demonstrates his own love for us in this: While we were still sinners, Christ died for us" (Romans 5:8). Because of Jesus' sacrifice, God meets each of us in our brokenness. He offers grace and redemption for those who trust in Him.

In this week's study, you will reflect on this all-important choice to seek out the Lord in *all* situations, assured that His grace is sufficient for your every need.

1. *How do you think God views you? His thoughts are higher than your own (see Isaiah 55:9), but what thoughts do you imagine He has about you?*

2. *What gets in the way of you believing that forgiveness is at the core of God's Presence? What helps you to believe it?*

Experience

I AM PLEASED WITH YOU, MY CHILD. Allow yourself to become fully aware of My pleasure shining upon you. You don't have to perform well in order to receive My Love. In fact, a performance focus will pull you away from Me, toward some sort of Pharisaism. This can be a subtle form of idolatry: worshiping your own good works. It can also be a source of deep discouragement when your works don't measure up to your expectations.

Shift your focus from your performance to My radiant Presence. The Light of My Love shines on you continually, regardless of your feelings or behavior. Your responsibility is to be receptive to this unconditional Love. Thankfulness and trust are your primary receptors. Thank Me for everything; *trust in Me at all times*. These simple disciplines will keep you open to My loving Presence.

– From *Jesus Calling*, November 20

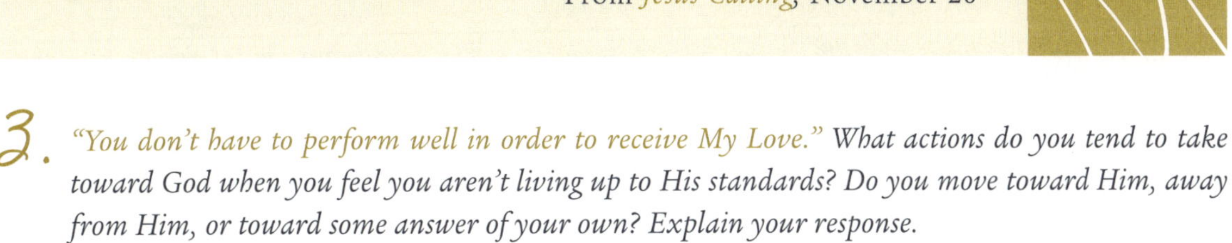

3. *"You don't have to perform well in order to receive My Love." What actions do you tend to take toward God when you feel you aren't living up to His standards? Do you move toward Him, away from Him, or toward some answer of your own? Explain your response.*

4. *"Shift your focus . . . to My radiant Presence." What helps you focus on God's radiant Presence rather than your own performance when you feel that you aren't living up to His standards? Or what might help you to focus on His Presence during such moments?*

Dwell

Read Luke 5:1–11. Consider how Peter (called Simon in this passage) reacted when he realized that he was in the presence of the Light of the world. As you read, keep in mind that fishing in the Lake of Gennesaret (the Sea of Galilee) was normally done at night. In the morning, the nets were carefully washed to remove debris, which was a time-consuming process.

5. *What was Peter's response when Jesus told him to go back out into the sea and cast the nets again? What does it say about Peter that he was willing to obey Christ?*

6. *Why did Peter say, "Go away from me, Lord; I am a sinful man!" (verse 8)? How typical do you think his response was to others who experienced Jesus' Presence?*

7. *Notice that Jesus did not say, "Peter, you have to clean yourself up first before you can receive My Love." What does this say about how Jesus receives you?*

8. *Jesus also did not say, "No, Peter, you're not a sinful man." Instead, what was Jesus' attitude toward Peter's admission of sinfulness? How does this response encourage you?*

Apply

The focus of this week's readings is on entering into God's Presence as a forgiven person. Jesus' sacrifice on the cross means your sins can be forgiven and your heart wiped clean! This is not because of anything *you've* done but solely because of *God's* Love and grace. Each day this week, take time to read the passage slowly and reflect on the truths being shared. Remember, again, this is your chance to connect with Jesus personally.

Day 1

Pray Psalm 139:1–6 aloud slowly. *What does the Lord know about you? Are you glad that He knows you this intimately . . . or is it a little intimidating? Why?*

Day 2

Read Psalm 139:1–6 again. *Choose a line, phrase, or just a word that jumps out at you. What is it about that line or word that touches you? How will you respond to it?*

Day 3

Read Psalm 139:7–12. *What is it like for you to be in Jesus' intimate Presence today? Do you eagerly rush toward Him or are you inclined to hide from Him? How easy is it for you to believe that He is here with you today? Explain your response.*

Day 4

Read Ephesians 2:8–10. *Read this passage once more and look for uses of the words* grace, faith, *and* works. *One by one, write down what role each of these words plays in your life.*

Day 5

Look again at what Paul writes in Ephesians 2:8–9. *Now write out a prayer to God, telling Him what you are thinking about grace, faith, and works in your life.*

Day 6

Read Romans 5:1–5 twice. *Close your eyes and picture yourself having access by faith into this grace in which every believer stands. Imagine grace as a throne room and you're standing there with complete access. Where is Jesus in this picture? Where is God the Father? What would you like to say to Them?*

Day 7

Read Luke 5:12–13. *Imagine yourself as someone witnessing this scene. What do you feel when the leper falls on the ground and begs for healing? When Jesus touches him? Do you relate most to the leper's illness, his begging, or his healing? Why?*

Week 3

LONGING FOR GOD'S LOVE

DISCOVER

When our trials seem insurmountable, we don't just long for God's Presence; we long for the certainty of His Love. We want to know, beyond a shadow of a doubt, that we are seen and deeply cherished by Him.

His boundless Love offers this assurance. In times of confusion, doubt, or overwhelming difficulty, God's Love constantly invites us closer, promising the quiet strength we need to endure and overcome our struggles. Empty substitutes or worldly alternatives can seem alluring at first, but what we really need is a love that speaks to the depths of our soul. A love that reaches for us even before we ask.

In this week's study, you will reflect on actively looking for the comfort and hope that God's Love alone brings to your most desperate moments.

1. *In times of stress or conflict, our natural bent is to either put up a fight or to flee from what is troubling us. Which of these responses comes more naturally to you? Why?*

2. *Is there something else you do instead? If so, what is it that you do?*

Experience

THERE IS NO PLACE so desolate that you cannot find Me there. When Hagar fled from her mistress, Sarah, into the wilderness, she thought she was utterly alone and forsaken. But Hagar encountered Me in that desolate place. There she addressed Me as *the Living One who sees me*. Through that encounter with My Presence, she gained courage to return to her mistress.

No set of circumstances could ever isolate you from My loving Presence. Not only do I see you always; I see you as a redeemed saint, gloriously radiant in My righteousness. That is why *I take great delight in you and rejoice over you with singing!*

— From *Jesus Calling*, August 30

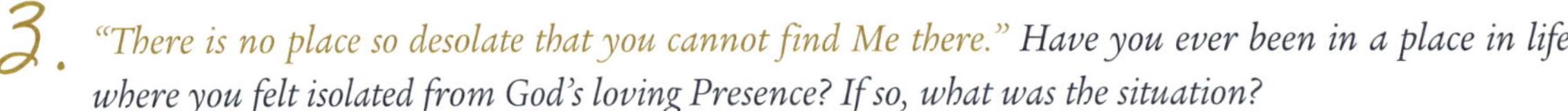

3. *"There is no place so desolate that you cannot find Me there." Have you ever been in a place in life where you felt isolated from God's loving Presence? If so, what was the situation?*

4. *"I see you always." Looking back, can you now see that God's Presence was with you even in the midst of that desolate situation? In other words, can you now recognize hints or outright signs of His Presence that you did not recognize back then?*

Dwell

Read Genesis 16:7–13. Sarai (later renamed Sarah), the wife of Abraham, had been unable to have children, so she convinced Abraham to have a child through Hagar, her maidservant. This method was customary at that time, and Sarai hoped she and Abraham would be able to build a family through her maidservant. Hagar did get pregnant, but then she became insolent toward Sarai. Sarai, in turn, became angry and envious. She mistreated Hagar—which probably means she had her whipped or beaten—so Hagar ran away into the desert. It was there, in that desolate place where "she thought she was utterly alone and forsaken," that God found her.

5. *Why do you think God asked Hagar where she had come from and where she was going? How did God reveal that He was about to change her identity and rewrite her story?*

6. *Hagar's response to this encounter was to address God as the Living "One who sees me" (verse 13). What does this reveal that she understood about the Lord?*

7. *Hagar realized the Lord Himself had been present with her. What does this story say about God's desire to be present with you? What does it say about His Love?*

8. *God sent Hagar back to the same circumstances from which she had fled. How do you respond to that reality? How do you think this encounter with God's Presence gave her the courage to return to Sarai—the one who had mistreated her?*

Apply

The focus of this week's readings is on consciously looking for indicators of God's Love, especially when you're feeling desperate. Each day, read the passage slowly, reflecting on the truths being shared. Remember, this is a chance to connect with Jesus and experience His Love.

Day 1

Read Romans 8:22–25 twice. *What does this passage say Christians should hope for? How easy is it for you to hope for what you don't see?*

Day 2

Read Romans 8:26–27. *What is a situation that you don't know how to pray about? How do you need the Holy Spirit to intercede for you in the midst of it?*

Day 3

Read Romans 8:28–30. *Is there an area of your life where you are finding it hard to see God working for your good or the good of someone you love? If so, what area? Where does His Love seem absent?*

Day 4

Read Romans 8:31–32. *What reasons do these verses offer God's people for being confident even in the face of suffering?*

Day 5

Read Romans 8:33–34. *How does it help you to know that Jesus is praying for you right now?*

Day 6

Read Romans 8:35–39. *What does this passage say about God's Presence for those who believe in Him?*

Day 7

Read Romans 8:35–39 again. *Which circumstances tend to make you feel separated from the Love of God? What are the ways this passage reassures you that God loves you and is present with you?*

Week 4

FINDING SAFETY IN CHRIST

Discover

Some days anxiety, our unwelcome companion, gets too close for comfort. Whether we are worried about finances, work, our health, or the well-being of our loved ones or community, fear often finds its way into our hearts.

Whatever shape those fears take, one thing is certain: We all feel afraid from time to time. But even in the moments when fear is threatening to overtake us, we can find comfort and renewed confidence in knowing that God is with us, holding us close. His Presence offers what this world can never provide: an unshakable safety.

In this week's study, you will explore the foundational truth that no matter what you're facing, you can rest securely in the steadfast Presence and perfect Peace of God.

1. *When you were a child, what were some of the things you were afraid of? How many of these fears, if any, have you carried over into adulthood?*

2. *As an adult, what is one thing you worry about or one thing that gives you a zing of fear?*

Experience

WHENEVER YOU FEEL DISTANT from Me, whisper My Name in loving trust. This simple prayer can restore your awareness of My Presence.

My Name is constantly abused in the world, where people use it as a curse word. This verbal assault reaches all the way to heaven; every word is heard and recorded. When you trustingly whisper My Name, My aching ears are soothed. The grating rancor of the world's blasphemies cannot compete with a trusting child's utterance: "Jesus." The power of My Name to bless both you and Me is beyond your understanding.

– From *Jesus Calling*, July 12

3. *"Whenever you feel distant from Me, whisper My Name." How does the thought that Jesus delights to hear you whisper His name as a prayer affect you and your view of Him?*

4. *"Trustingly whisper My Name." What will you have to overcome to build a habit of whispering Jesus' Name throughout the day? What will it take for you to overcome this?*

Dwell

Read Matthew 8:23–27 and consider the power of the disciples' "simple prayer" in this story. Focus on Jesus sleeping soundly in the fishing boat as the storm raged around Him while the disciples were overwhelmed with fear and expressed a lack of faith in Him. As you read, note the Sea of Galilee was known for sudden and violent storms, often triggered by changes in temperatures and wind patterns. These storms could quickly escalate from calm to dangerous.

5. *How would you describe the way the disciples spoke Jesus' Name in this story? What does this reveal about their lack of trust in Him in this situation?*

6. *Why did Jesus say the disciples had "little faith" when He awoke (verse 26)? What would great faith have looked like in this situation?*

7. *Are you in a "storm"? If so, what would great faith look like for you in the midst of it?*

8. *What does this story reveal about the power of calling on Jesus' Name in the midst of your storms? What does it look like for you to "trustingly whisper" His Name?*

Apply

The focus of this week's readings is on finding safety in Jesus' Presence. Each day, read the passage slowly, pausing to think about what is being said and to reflect on the truths being shared. Remember, this is an opportunity to rest in the Presence and Peace of God.

Day 1

Read Psalm 116:1–6. *Which emotions does the psalmist express? Where do you see his desperation?*

Day 2

Read Psalm 116:1–6 again. *What do you think is involved in calling on the Name of the Lord beyond simply speaking the word? What attitudes and actions might be involved?*

Day 3

Read Psalm 148:1–6, 13. *What reasons do you have for praising God?*

Day 4

Read Psalm 31:1–5. *What does the psalmist ask for as it relates to "the trap" (verse 4) that is set for him? What are you moved to ask for when you find yourself in similar situations?*

Day 5

Read Psalm 7:1–5. *Why does the psalmist invite the Lord to look at his actions and point out any guilt? How easy is it for you to claim guiltlessness in God's eyes?*

Day 6

Read Matthew 20:28. *Recall what Jesus has done for you. How does that recollection help you deal with condemning voices?*

Day 7

Read Exodus 33:12–20. *What is one thing you especially want to ask God to provide for you?*

Week 5

APPROACHING GOD WITH AWE

Discover

What a profound comfort God's Presence is for those who truly rely on Him! He approaches us with gentleness and compassion, offering peace and solace when we need them most. He is also the Lord Almighty, the Ultimate Authority, the Creator of the universe. To experience His Presence is to reverently and humbly remember that we tread on holy ground.

This is one of the beautiful mysteries of the Christian faith: that a holy and just God would care so much about His people that He would make Himself personal and accessible. He wants to be intimately known and joyfully worshiped.

In this week's study, you will concentrate on experiencing God in the splendor of His holiness. To begin, you will reflect on your earthly father, as your understanding of your earthly father will often shape how you relate to your heavenly Father.

1. *What was your father like when you were a child? Was he someone you went to when you scraped your knee? Was he someone you looked up to? Did he scare you? Was he absent?*

2. *The psalmist wrote, "Let all the inhabitants of the world stand in awe of [God]" (Psalm 33:8 ESV). What is awe? When, if ever, have you felt awe?*

Experience

Come to Me and listen! Attune yourself to My voice, and receive My richest blessings. Marvel at the wonder of communing with the Creator of the universe while sitting in the comfort of your home. Kings who reign on earth tend to make themselves inaccessible; ordinary people almost never gain an audience with them. Even dignitaries must plow through red tape and protocol in order to speak with royalty.

Though I am King of the universe, I am totally accessible to you. I am with you wherever you are. Nothing can separate you from My Presence! When I cried out from the cross, "It is finished!" *the curtain of the temple was torn in two from top to bottom.* This opened the way for you to meet Me face-to-Face, with no need of protocol or priests. I, the King of kings, am your constant Companion.

— From *Jesus Calling*, September 26

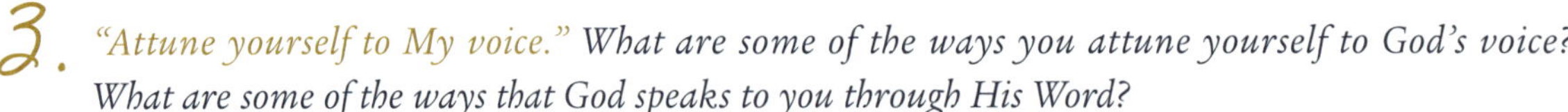

3. *"Attune yourself to My voice." What are some of the ways you attune yourself to God's voice? What are some of the ways that God speaks to you through His Word?*

4. *"I am with you wherever you are." Have you begun to experience God as your constant Companion? If so, what has that changed for you? If not, do you have any greater sense of His Presence now that you're meeting with Him regularly face-to-Face?*

Dwell

Read Isaiah 6:1–8. This passage tells the story of Isaiah entering the temple in Jerusalem and having his first-ever vision of God. In the vision, Isaiah sees several seraphim (a type of angel), and God calls him to be a prophet and speak His words to Israel. Think of how you are able to meet with the "King of the universe," who is also "totally accessible to you," as you read.

5. *Isaiah was an ordinary human being, yet the King of the universe chose to reveal Himself to him and commune with him. Why do you think the Lord gave Isaiah this vision of His throne? What was He revealing to his soon-to-be prophet about His power and glory?*

6. *Why did Isaiah say, "I am ruined" (verse 5) when he saw this vision from the Lord? What do you think he was afraid was going to happen?*

7. *Isaiah knew that a man with "unclean lips" (verse 5) was unprepared to be in the Presence of the holy God. What do you think it means to have "unclean lips"? Why did a "live coal" (verse 6) from the altar of sacrifice take away Isaiah's guilt?*

8. *When Jesus "gave up his spirit" and died on the cross, the curtain of the temple was "torn in two from top to bottom" (Matthew 27:50–51). This curtain separated the Holy of Holies (the earthly dwelling place of God's Presence) from the rest of the temple. What was God saying about who could meet with Him face-to-Face—without the protocol or priests?*

Apply

The focus of this week's readings is on approaching God's Presence with awe. Each day, read the passage slowly, pausing to think about what is being said. Remember, this is your opportunity to meet face-to-Face with the King of the universe.

Day 1

Read Exodus 3:1–6. *What were God's instructions to Moses when he approached the bush? What do you learn about holiness in this story?*

Day 2

Read Exodus 3:1–6 again. *Why was Moses afraid to look at God? How does the realization that this same God invites you into His Presence impact you? What do you want to say to God today?*

Day 3

Read Exodus 3:7–9. *How easy is it for you to conceive of a God who is both awe-inspiring and caring? Is this a God you want to draw close to? Why or why not?*

Day 4

Read Psalm 29:1–9. *Why would the psalmist use* thunder *and* lightning *to describe the Lord? What is good about serving a God like this? Is this a God you are drawn to? Why or why not?*

Day 5

Read Isaiah 55:1–3. *What are you thirsty for? In what ways does the Lord's Presence satisfy what you're hungry and thirsty for?*

Day 6

Read Isaiah 55:1–3 again. *What are the things you've labored for that don't satisfy? What would you like to do differently?*

Day 7

Read Isaiah 55:6–9. *Do you have any unrighteous ways or thoughts that you need to turn away from? If so, what are they? What do you need to say to God about them?*

Week 6

FACING GRIEF

Discover

Anytime we lose someone or something we hold dear, grief follows in its wake. The waves of sorrow don't only accompany the death of someone we love. The loss of a job, a marriage, our home, our health, or a beloved pet comes with its own set of tears and sadness as well.

The heartbreak can feel overwhelming, and God may seem distant. Meanwhile, His comforting Presence is closer than we realize. Because Jesus deeply understands our pain, He doesn't just witness our suffering from afar; He walks beside us as we go through it, offering compassion, peace, and hope through His Spirit.

This week's study invites you to discover God's constant, consoling Presence and divine empathy in the midst of your grief and heartache.

1. *What would you say has been the most significant loss you've endured in your life? Briefly describe the situation and what you went through.*

2. *How did you cope with the loss? Did you "pull yourself together" and move on? Did you talk to someone you trust? Did you withdraw? Explain your response.*

Experience

Do not expect to be treated fairly in this life. People will say and do hurtful things to you, things that you don't deserve. When someone mistreats you, try to view it as an opportunity to grow in grace. See how quickly you can forgive the one who has wounded you. Don't be concerned about setting the record straight. Instead of obsessing about other people's opinions of you, keep your focus on Me. Ultimately, it is My view of you that counts.

As you concentrate on relating to Me, remember that I have clothed you in My righteousness and holiness. I see you attired in these radiant garments, which I bought for you with My blood. This also is not fair; it is pure gift. When others treat you unfairly, remember that My ways with you are much better than fair. My ways are Peace and *Love, which I have poured out into your heart by My Spirit.*

— From *Jesus Calling*, October 28

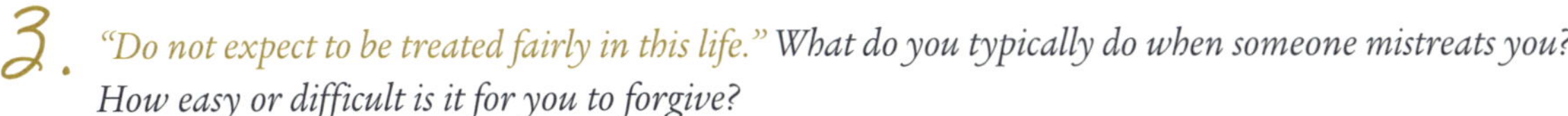

3. *"Do not expect to be treated fairly in this life." What do you typically do when someone mistreats you? How easy or difficult is it for you to forgive?*

4. *"When someone mistreats you, try to view it as an opportunity to grow in grace." Do you think this would be possible for you to do? Why or why not? What would have to change for you to be able to view mistreatment as an opportunity to grow in grace?*

Dwell

Read John 19:17–27 and consider that when others treat you unfairly, "[God's] ways with you are much better than fair." As you read, note that crucifixion in the first century was a common (and agonizing) method of execution the Romans employed for any "enemy" of the state. John relates that in Jesus' crucifixion, the soldiers stripped Him (to humiliate Him) and then nailed Him to a cross at His wrists and ankles. These events took place after Judas, one of the twelve disciples, betrayed Christ (see Mark 14:10). Meanwhile, Jesus' mother, some other women, and "the disciple whom [Jesus] loved" (verse 26)—likely John himself—looked on. All the other male disciples were hiding (see Mark 14:50), afraid they too would be arrested.

5. *Jesus was the sinless Son of God. How would you describe the way He was treated unfairly in this story? How was He treated unfairly by even His close disciples (see Mark 14:10, 50)?*

6. *What do you think this experience must have been like for Jesus' loved ones who were at the cross? What would it take to hang on to faith in God in this situation?*

7. *What does this story reveal about any expectations you might have about being treated fairly in this life? What does it reveal about the importance of being able to forgive?*

8. *When you are treated unfairly, what helps you to remember that God's ways with you are "much better than fair"? What "unfair" benefits have you received because of God's grace?*

Apply

The focus of this week's readings is on depending on God during seasons of grief and sorrow. Each day, read the passage slowly, pausing to think about what is being said. Remember, this is an opportunity to discover God's consoling Presence and divine empathy.

Day 1

Read Luke 23:32–43. *How did the two men on the crosses near Jesus respond to Him? In what ways was Jesus' Presence comforting to the man who understood his guilt?*

Day 2

Read Luke 23:32–43 again. *Jesus was merciful even in His moment of greatest loss. How does loss affect your ability to forgive others?*

Day 3

Read Luke 23:48–56. *How did the people who gathered to witness Jesus' execution respond to His death? How did Joseph of Arimathea and the faithful women followers react? If you've lost a loved one, how does this scene affect you?*

Day 4

Read Psalm 22:1–5. *Look for any words in these verses that speak to your current situation. Which words did you choose? Why did you choose those words?*

Day 5

Read Psalm 22:1–5 again. *How easy is it for you to be this honest with God? Tell God whatever this psalm moves you to say.*

Day 6

Read Psalm 22:1. *Jesus quoted the first line of this psalm when He hung on the cross (see Mark 15:34). In the culture of the time, quoting the first line was a way of referring to the entire psalm. Why was this an appropriate psalm for Jesus to be thinking of on the cross?*

Day 7

Read Psalm 22:25–31. *How does it affect you to think of Jesus in connection with this psalm?*

Week 7

DEATH IS DEFEATED

Discover

On one extraordinary morning in history, the impossible happened: Death was defeated once and for all. Jesus triumphed over sin, evil, the cross, and the grave, giving us an enduring reminder of God's constancy, closeness, redemption, and resurrection power.

This momentous event—Christ's victory over the grave—changed *everything*, both then and now. No matter how insurmountable our obstacles might seem, or crushing our grief might feel, we can resoundingly trust the Lord never abandons us. Because Jesus lives, He is in the difficulty with us. He walks beside us, gently and patiently guiding us through the darkness and pain that we are enduring.

In this study, you will reflect on that miraculous resurrection morning and explore how it ensures God's Presence in the face of life's most difficult challenges.

1. *How has your awareness of God's Presence changed since the beginning of this 52-week study? How close or distant does Jesus seem to you right now?*

2. *How has the habit you've been building (or reinforcing) of regularly spending time with God affected your awareness of His Presence?*

Experience

I AM ALL AROUND YOU, hovering over you even as you seek My Face. I am nearer than you dare believe, closer than the air you breathe. If My children could only recognize My Presence, they would never feel lonely again. *I know every thought before you think it, every word before you speak it.* My Presence impinges on your innermost being. Can you see the absurdity of trying to hide anything from Me? You can easily deceive other people, and even yourself, but I read you like an open, large-print book.

Deep within themselves, most people have some awareness of My imminent Presence. Many people run from Me and vehemently deny My existence because My closeness terrifies them. But My own children have nothing to fear, for I have cleansed them by My blood and clothed them in My righteousness. Be blessed by My intimate nearness. Since I live in you, let Me also live through you, shining My Light into the darkness.

– From *Jesus Calling*, August 24

3. *"I am nearer than you dare believe." Why might Jesus' closeness terrify a person?*

4. *"I know every thought before you think it." Does the truth of this statement bring you comfort? Or does it terrify you? Explain your response.*

Dwell

Read John 20:11–18. Mary Magdalene was a follower of Jesus for much of His ministry. He drove seven demons from her, and in gratitude she supported His ministry financially (see Luke 8:1–3). Mary was one of the women who witnessed His crucifixion. She went to Jesus' tomb at dawn to finish the burial rites (see 24:1), but when she found it empty, she assumed someone had stolen the body (see John 20:1–2). After reporting the missing body of Jesus to the disciples, she returned to the empty tomb to grieve. It was a dark time for her, but Jesus was about to shine His "Light into the darkness" and reveal His Presence to her.

5. *What was Mary's state of mind when she saw Jesus' tomb was empty—and assumed somebody had taken His body? What changed when she realized that Jesus was nearer than she "dare believe" and "closer than the air" she breathed?*

6. *Jesus said to Mary, "Do not hold on to me" (verse 17), which indicates she had taken hold of His hands or thrown herself at His feet. Why did she do this? What was she expressing? What tone of voice do you think Jesus used with Mary when He told her not to cling to Him?*

7. *Would it be hard for you to not "hold on" to an experience of Jesus' Presence like this? Why or why not? How difficult would it have been for you to leave this moment and follow Jesus' instructions to "go instead to [His] brothers" (verse 17)?*

8. *Many people run from Christ and are terrified of His closeness. What does Mary's example reveal about the way God's children* should *respond to His nearness?*

Apply

The focus of this week's readings is on experiencing the Presence of the resurrected Jesus, the Son of God. Each day, read the passage slowly, pausing to think about and reflect on what is being said. Remember, this is an opportunity to meet with the risen Christ.

Day 1

Read Luke 24:13–27. *Why do you think Jesus didn't make Himself known to the two men immediately? Why did He make Himself known by explaining the Old Testament scriptures?*

Day 2

Read Luke 24:28–45. *Why do you think Jesus made Himself known to the two disciples in that moment of taking bread, blessing it, breaking it, and giving it?*

Day 3

Read Luke 22:19, *which is from Luke's account of Jesus' last meal with His disciples before His crucifixion. How does Jesus make Himself known in your life?*

Day 4

Read Luke 24:36–44. *What would it be like to touch Jesus, even His wounds? What do you feel as this scene unfolds? How does your reaction resemble that of the disciples? How does it differ from theirs?*

Day 5

Read Luke 24:45–48. *How does Jesus summarize the gospel message? How do His words affect you?*

Day 6

Read Luke 24:45–48 again. *What does "repentance for the forgiveness of sins" (verse 47) mean to you? How do Jesus' words affect you?*

Day 7

Read John 20:24–29. *How often do you believe without seeing? How does the lack of seeing affect your faith in Jesus' Presence? Speak honestly with Jesus about this.*

Week 8

JESUS' CONTINUING PRESENCE

DISCOVER

Jesus was bodily present on earth for thirty-three years, sharing His life with His disciples, who spent nearly three years in close fellowship with Him. But the time came when they had to trust His *spiritual* Presence rather than His *physical* one—a challenge that resonates with us today.

Jesus calls us to place our trust not in what we see but in the certainty of His spiritual nearness. His nearness is guaranteed by the Holy Spirit, who dwells in the heart of every believer. And Jesus Himself is interceding for us in the throne room of heaven.

In this week's study, you will join the disciples as Jesus encourages them to press in to His enduring spiritual Presence. This is a Presence that continues to guide you and comfort you each day, in every step you take, across the entire course of your life.

1. *Put yourself in the place of Jesus' disciples. What are some of the benefits they received from being* physically *present with Jesus during His ministry?*

2. *What do you think went through the disciples' minds when they learned that Jesus would not always be physically present with them? What questions do you think they had?*

Experience

Look to Me continually for help, comfort, and companionship. Because I am always by your side, the briefest glance can connect you with Me. When you look to Me for help, it flows freely from My Presence. This recognition of your need for Me, in small matters as well as in large ones, keeps you spiritually alive.

When you need comfort, I love to enfold you in My arms. I enable you not only to feel comforted but also to be a channel through whom I comfort others. Thus, you are doubly blessed, because a living channel absorbs some of whatever flows through it.

My constant Companionship is the *pièce de résistance*: the summit of salvation blessings. No matter what losses you experience in your life, no one can take away this glorious gift.

— From *Jesus Calling*, October 16

3. *"When you look to Me for help, it flows freely from My Presence." Do you find this to be true in your life? If so, how do you experience His help? If not, what gets in the way?*

4. *"When you need comfort, I love to enfold you in My arms." What are some ways Jesus has comforted you? How has He allowed you to be a vessel through whom He comforts others?*

Dwell

Read Matthew 28:16–20. Matthew relates that Jesus appeared in bodily form to His eleven disciples after His resurrection and would soon send the Holy Spirit to dwell inside them. Christ was, in effect, preparing them for the transition from His physical Presence to His Presence in the Spirit. He was also preparing them for the great work that He would give to them. Consider the promise Jesus makes to His disciples—"surely I am with you always, to the very end of the age" (verse 20)—and reflect on the implications of this promise to you.

5. *Imagine yourself being with Jesus, receiving these instructions. Would you have had wholehearted faith? Or would you likely have doubted His words? Why do you think Matthew made a point of telling us that some of the disciples doubted Jesus?*

6. *What role do you personally have in Jesus' command to His followers to "go and make disciples . . . baptizing them . . . and teaching them to obey [Him]" (verses 19–20)?*

7. *Jesus' promise to His disciples was His constant companionship. No matter what losses they would face after His departure from earth—and they would face many—no one could take away this glorious gift. Where in your own life have you sensed this "with you" Presence most clearly? How has Jesus' constant Presence been a gift in your life?*

8. *Are you in a season of life right now where being a comfort to others feels like too much? If so, how does Jesus' promise of companionship—to be with you in work that He has given you to do—help you do this with joy?*

Apply

The focus of this week's readings is on considering Jesus' call to reflect the ongoing Light of His Presence to others. Each day, read the passage slowly, pausing to think about what is being said. Remember, this is your invitation to experience Jesus' enduring Presence in your life.

Day 1

Read John 15:1–5. *What does it mean to remain connected to Jesus? How do you cultivate that connection?*

Day 2

Reread John 15:1–5, and then read 15:12–13. *What is the fruit that comes from being connected with Jesus and abiding (or remaining) in Him? What effort does that fruit require on your part? What effort does it require from Jesus?*

Day 3

Read Matthew 7:16–20. *As a believer, do you ever have feelings of failure about not bearing enough fruit? What do you think Jesus thinks about those feelings? Does He see you as a failure, or does He celebrate what He is doing in you? Explain your response.*

Day 4

Read John 17:13–24. *This is part of a long prayer that Jesus prayed to the Father for His disciples. Go through each request and ask the Father to do what Jesus asked for you. Which requests stand out as being most important for you right now? Why those requests?*

Day 5

Read 1 Corinthians 1:10. *Why is oneness among God's people so important to the Lord? What does such unity communicate to the world?*

Day 6

Read John 20:19–23. *What did the Father send Jesus to do? What does Jesus send His disciples to do? Why was (and is) the Holy Spirit necessary for this?*

Day 7

Read Matthew 5:14–16. *How is it possible to be the light of the world in the place you're in?*

Week 9

NO WORRIES!

Discover

Scripture reminds us of a profound and unwavering truth: *God is perfectly faithful*. Unlike anything or anyone else we may have counted on in the past, His trustworthiness has no limits. God never falters, never overlooks us, and never fails us.

This absolute reliability may be impossible for us to believe—especially if our hearts have been broken by disappointment. Years of being let down by others can diminish our belief that God not only stands ready to handle every challenge we face but also that He will actually do it. Yet it is precisely His steadfast nature that makes Him worthy of all our trust.

In this week's study, as you dig into the promises of God found in His Word, the challenge is for you to begin tearing down any barriers of mistrust in Him that you have erected in your life. You truly *can* rely on the One who is unfailing, unchanging, and forever true.

1. *On a typical day, how consistently do you relax and trust in God's strength?*

2. *What about today? What helped you trust God? What got in the way?*

Experience

Strive to trust Me in more and more areas of your life. Anything that tends to make you anxious is a growth opportunity. Instead of running away from these challenges, embrace them, eager to gain all the blessings I have hidden in the difficulties. If you believe that I am sovereign over every aspect of your life, it is possible to trust Me in all situations. Don't waste energy regretting the way things are or thinking about what might have been. Start at the present moment—accepting things exactly as they are—and search for My way in the midst of those circumstances.

Trust is like a staff you can lean on as you journey uphill with Me. If you are trusting in Me consistently, the staff will bear as much of your weight as needed. *Lean on, trust, and be confident in Me with all your heart and mind.*

— From *Jesus Calling*, January 22

3. *"Strive to trust Me in more and more areas of your life." What are some areas in your life where you find it difficult to trust God? What sorts of things do you get anxious about?*

4. *"Trust is like a staff you can lean on." What approach do you typically take when you are facing an uphill journey? What are ways you are actively leaning on God right now?*

Dwell

Read Matthew 6:25–34. Jesus spoke these words to a group of people who were under the rule of the mighty Roman Empire. Uncertainties and anxieties were just a part of their everyday life. Yet Jesus instructed them *not* to worry because there was a greater Power in control—One who cared deeply about them. Jesus was, in effect, saying to them (and us), "If you believe that I am sovereign over every aspect of your life, it is possible to trust Me in all situations."

5. *What are some examples Jesus uses of the kinds of things that people worry about? What reasons does He give for not worrying about those things?*

6. *Jesus says the "pagans run after all these things" (verse 32), which means those who trust God is sovereign run after other things—namely, His righteousness. What is the promise Jesus gives for those who choose to seek after God's kingdom and righteousness first?*

7. *What do you think of the idea of saying "I trust You, Jesus" in response to every need that comes up in your life? How might that help you to trust in Him more?*

8. *When you consider how you typically respond to worry-inducing situations, can you honestly say you believe God is in sovereign control over every aspect of your life? If not, what would need to change for you to truly believe this moment by moment in everyday situations?*

Apply

The focus of this week's readings is on letting go of worry and trusting in God. Each day, read the passage slowly, pausing to consider what is being said. Remember, this is your opportunity to learn how to rely on the One who is unfailing, unchanging, and forever true.

Day 1

Read Proverbs 2:1–22. *Why is it unwise to rely on your own understanding? Give an example.*

Day 2

Read Proverbs 3:5–6. *What path are you currently most concerned about? Are you tempted to worry about it? How could trusting in God's sovereignty in that situation help you?*

Day 3

Read Psalm 37:1–6. *What does it mean to "fret" (verse 1)? What reasons does the psalmist provide for why you shouldn't fret?*

Day 4

Read Psalm 37:7. *What does it mean for you to "be still before the Lord" and "wait patiently" when things are uncertain? How does trusting in God enable you to do this?*

Day 5

Read Isaiah 40:10–11. *Why is it important to know that God "comes with power" when it comes to trusting in Him? How does thinking about this aspect of His character affect your anxiety?*

Day 6

Read Psalm 23:1–4. *Picture yourself walking through "the darkest valley" (verse 4) and being comforted and strengthened rather than afraid. How does this image impact the way you see the situations you are most tempted to worry about?*

Day 7

Read Psalm 127:1–2. *What does the psalmist say about anxious toil in this passage? How is it different from hard work without anxiety?*

Week 10

WHEN YOU PRAY

Discover

How do you imagine God when you pray? Is He leaning in, listening intently, His eyes full of love and His heart completely focused on you? Or do you perceive Him as only half listening—or maybe even inconvenienced or angry?

The way you envision God profoundly shapes your prayers. It influences your confidence to share your needs, the persistence with which you seek Him, and your level of trust in His care and provision. Knowing that God listens with love can absolutely transform the way you approach Him, deepening your relationship and strengthening your faith.

In this week's study, you will explore a parable Jesus shared that reveals God's attentive and compassionate nature. Through this story, you will be encouraged to see God as the loving, openhearted, and responsive Father that He truly is.

1. *Think of a difficulty in your life. How could it encourage you to depend more on God? What would that dependence look like?*

2. *Do you trust God enough to depend on Him in this situation you've identified? What encourages you to trust Him? What, if anything, discourages you?*

Experience

I AM ABLE *to do far beyond all that you ask or imagine.* Come to Me with positive expectations, knowing that there is no limit to what I can accomplish. Ask My Spirit to control your mind so that you can think great thoughts of Me. Do not be discouraged by the fact that many of your prayers are yet unanswered. Time is a trainer, teaching you to wait upon Me, to trust Me in the dark. The more extreme your circumstances, the more likely you are to see *My Power and Glory* at work in the situation. Instead of letting difficulties draw you into worrying, try to view them as setting the scene for My glorious intervention. Keep your eyes and your mind wide open to all that I am doing in your life.

– From *Jesus Calling*, January 6

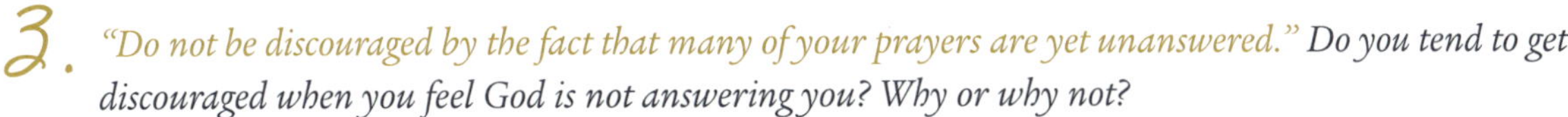

3. *"Do not be discouraged by the fact that many of your prayers are yet unanswered." Do you tend to get discouraged when you feel God is not answering you? Why or why not?*

4. *"Time is a trainer, teaching you to wait upon Me." How has this been true in your life? What reasons do you have for trusting in God while you wait for an answer—and which of those particular reasons seem especially motivating to you?*

Dwell

Read Luke 18:1–8 as you reflect on the idea of keeping "your eyes and your mind wide open to all that [Jesus is] doing in your life." In this passage, Jesus teaches the importance of holding fast to unwavering hope through persistent prayer. The parable highlights not only the power of prayer and faith but also God's responsiveness to us regardless of the trials we face.

5. *How is the judge in the parable like God? How is he different from God?*

6. *What is Jesus' point in comparing God to the judge in this parable? How does Jesus use this story to get at the way people tend to imagine God?*

7. *How did the widow respond when the judge did not immediately grant her request? What point was Jesus making about the importance of not getting "discouraged by the fact that many of your prayers are yet unanswered"?*

8. *What statement does Jesus make at the end of this passage about God's "justice for his chosen ones" (verse 7)? How might this parable be an encouragement to you during those times when God asks you to wait on Him and "trust [Him] in the dark"?*

Apply

The focus of this week's readings is on trusting the goodness of God and taking your needs to Him in prayer. Each day, read the passage slowly, pausing to think about what is being said. Remember, this is an opportunity to encounter God's attentive and compassionate nature.

Day 1

Read Luke 18:1–8 again. *Imagine yourself as the persistent widow making the same plea to the judge day after day. How long would it take for you to get tired of praying like this? What would you do if you had to pray this way for months before getting a response from God?*

Day 2

Read Luke 18:9–14. *How did the Pharisee's trust affect the results of his prayer? How did the tax collector's trust affect the results of his prayer?*

Day 3

Read Luke 18:9–14 again. *How is this story relevant to your own prayers? What do you want to say to God right now?*

Day 4

Read Psalm 6:1–10. *How would you describe David's emotions? Do those emotions fit with trust? Why or why not? What emotions do you need to take to God in prayer today?*

Day 5

Read Psalm 10:12–18. *What does the psalmist pray for? Can you identify with his words? If so, in what ways?*

Day 6

Read Psalm 18:1–6. *What can you take from this passage and incorporate into a prayer to God today—even if you don't yet have the thing you are praying for?*

Day 7

Read Psalm 61:1–8. *What does the psalmist ask for in prayer? Can you affirm any of his statements of trust? Or do you question whether those things are true in your case?*

Week 11

NEVER LOSE HEART

Discover

It's easy to trust God's Presence when everything in life is going well. But true faith is revealed when we face hardships and uncertainty and the futility of even our best efforts.

During times of pain and struggle that feel beyond our strength, we might wonder, *God, are You there? Do You really care about me and what I am going through?* Yet this is precisely when the Lord calls us to anchor our trust in Him. Instead of being tossed around by fear and worry or relying on our own strength, God urges us to cast our cares on Him.

In this week's study, you will explore how the apostle Paul found unwavering faith in God during a time of profound suffering. Paul offers a powerful example of what true dependence on the Lord looks like when you are faced with difficulties and obstacles.

1. *Make a list of some of your current struggles, both physically and emotionally.*

2. *How would you describe the level of trust and faith you're placing in God to carry you through the difficulties you've just identified?*

Experience

APPROACH PROBLEMS with a light touch. When your mind moves toward a problem area, you tend to focus on that situation so intensely that you lose sight of Me. You pit yourself against the difficulty as if you had to conquer it immediately. Your mind gears up for battle, and your body becomes tense and anxious. Unless you achieve total victory, you feel defeated.

There is a better way. When a problem starts to overshadow your thoughts, bring this matter to Me. Talk with Me about it and look at it in the Light of My Presence. This puts some much-needed space between you and your concern, enabling you to see from My perspective. You will be surprised at the results. Sometimes you may even laugh at yourself for being so serious about something so insignificant.

You will always face trouble in this life. But more importantly, you will always have Me with you, helping you to handle whatever you encounter. Approach problems with a light touch by viewing them in My revealing Light.

— From *Jesus Calling*, November 15

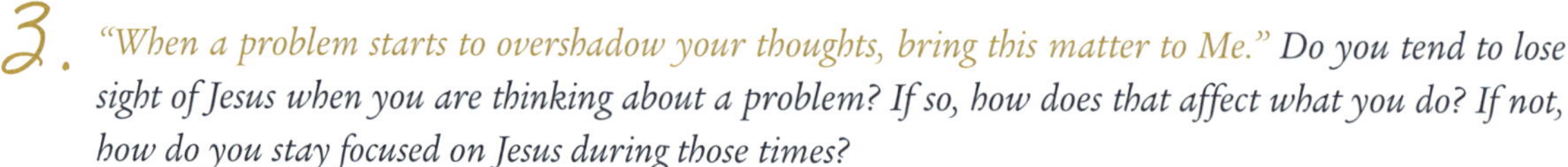

3. *"When a problem starts to overshadow your thoughts, bring this matter to Me." Do you tend to lose sight of Jesus when you are thinking about a problem? If so, how does that affect what you do? If not, how do you stay focused on Jesus during those times?*

4. *"You will always face trouble in this life." What would it take for you to develop a habit of* always *taking the troubles you face to Jesus? What would help you to do that?*

Dwell

Read 2 Corinthians 4:6–12, 16–18. In this passage, Paul emphasizes that "our light and momentary troubles are achieving for us an eternal glory that far outweighs them all" (verse 17). Suffering, Paul states, is temporary and will yield eternal glory—and in their weakness, Jesus would make God's power all the more evident.

5. *For Paul, the knowledge of God's glory wasn't mere information about Him but a deeper understanding of Him gained through personal experience. Has God given you the knowledge of His glory by similar means? If so, what difference has it made in your life?*

6. *Paul speaks of "treasure in jars of clay" (verse 7). What was that treasure? What was the effect of that treasure when Paul was faced with problems?*

7. *How does Paul describe the type of troubles his readers are facing? How do his words encourage you to look at the troubles you are facing "in the Light of [Jesus'] Presence"?*

8. *What does it mean for us to "fix our eyes not on what is seen, but on what is unseen" (verse 18)? How would that help you not to lose sight of Jesus in the midst of your troubles?*

Apply

The focus of this week's readings is on trusting in God when things are difficult. Each day, read the passage slowly, pausing to consider what is being said. Remember, this is an opportunity to meet with Jesus and learn what true dependence on Him means in times of trial.

Day 1

Read 2 Corinthians 1:8–11. *How serious was Paul's suffering? How did he describe it? What purpose did he see in his suffering? How did prayer help Paul?*

Day 2

Read John 11:25–26. *Does knowing that God raised Jesus from the dead increase your confidence in God? Why or why not?*

Day 3

Read Psalm 27:1–5. *What does it mean to call the Lord "my light"? What does it mean to call Him "the stronghold of my life" (verse 1)?*

Day 4

Read Psalm 27:1–5 again. *What is the psalmist confident the Lord will do for him? Does this mean nothing bad will ever happen to him? Explain your response.*

Day 5

Read Psalm 63:1–8. *How often do you thirst for God versus other things? Which other things arouse your thirst? What are a couple of ways you could return your focus to the Lord?*

Day 6

Read Psalm 91:1–8. *Make a list of the images the psalmist uses to describe the Lord. Picture these things in your mind, and then picture yourself finding safety there. Ask God to write one of these pictures on your heart to affirm the truth about who He is in your life.*

Day 7

Read Psalm 91:1–8 again, and then read verses 9–16. *In practical terms, how do you make the Lord your "refuge" and your "dwelling" (verse 9)?*

Week 12

A CRY FOR HELP

DISCOVER

In this week's study, you will meet a widow crying out for help. In God's response to her, you are given a poignant reminder of His deep compassion for all those who are in need.

Widows appear frequently in the Bible. They were often among the most vulnerable in their society, cast into desperate situations by limited opportunities and the loss of both the status and income their husbands provided. Yet time and again, Scripture shows God's heart for the most vulnerable and the numerous ways in which He provided for them.

These stories serve as a reminder of God's unwavering faithfulness and care for us, particularly in our helplessness. Through our struggles, God teaches us to cry out to Him for help, relying on Him for both provision and compassion.

1. *If you think of your life as a journey on foot through the mountains, how would you describe the portion of the path you are on right now? How rocky or smooth is it? How steep? How long has it been like this?*

2. *Are there recent situations when you have found yourself crying out to God for help? If so, how have you witnessed His response to your desperation?*

Experience

You need Me every moment. Your awareness of your constant need for Me is your greatest strength. Your neediness, properly handled, is a link to My Presence. However, there are pitfalls that you must be on guard against: self-pity, self-preoccupation, giving up. Your inadequacy presents you with a continual choice—deep dependence on Me or despair. The emptiness you feel within will be filled either with problems or with My Presence. Make Me central in your consciousness by *praying continually*: simple, short prayers flowing out of the present moment. Use My Name liberally, to remind you of My Presence. *Keep on asking and you will receive, so that your gladness may be full and complete.*

— From *Jesus Calling*, February 22

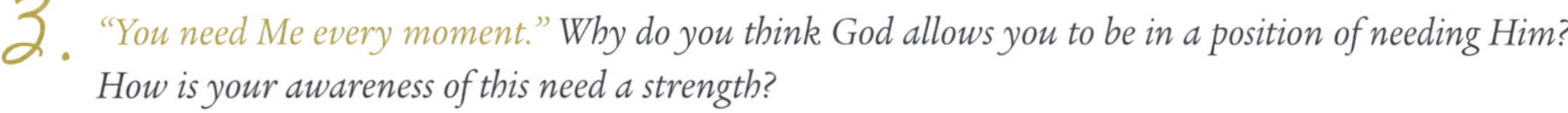

3. *"You need Me every moment." Why do you think God allows you to be in a position of needing Him? How is your awareness of this need a strength?*

4. *"Make Me central in your consciousness by praying continually." What are some examples of simple, short prayers that might flow out of the present moment you are in?*

Dwell

Read 2 Kings 4:1–7. This miraculous account from the life of the prophet Elisha paints a vivid picture of God's provision. During this time in Israel's history, creditors could enslave debtors and their children to work off a debt when they could not pay. This was the widow's situation, which left her with a choice: "Deep dependence on [God] or despair." Although God didn't do miracles like this every day, in this instance He chose to intervene through Elisha.

5. *The widow in this story knew that she was in dire need of the Lord's help. How did she handle that need? What did God ultimately reveal about His Presence to her?*

6. *What Elisha instructed the widow to do was simple but risky. What was she required to give up as a step of faith and trust in God? What step of faith is the Lord inviting you to take right now in your life that feels small but requires trust?*

7. *The widow was ultimately completely dependent on whatever the Lord would provide to help her. How have you dealt with great neediness and dependence in your life? What kinds of things do you tend to do when you are in great need?*

8. *The widow expressed a prayer to God "flowing out of the present moment." What goes through your mind when you think about crying out to God like this? Does that seem to be the right thing to do? Do you feel any resistance to doing this? Explain your response.*

Apply

The focus of this week's readings is on depending on God's provision to meet your deepest needs. Each day, read the passage slowly, pausing to think about what is being said. Remember, this is an opportunity to meet with Jesus and cry out to Him in your need.

Day 1

Read 2 Corinthians 12:7–10. *Why was Paul given a thorn in his flesh? Why didn't God take away the thorn?*

Day 2

Read 2 Corinthians 12:9–10 again. *What does it mean that God's power is "made perfect" in every Christian's weakness? Do you find it possible to mirror Paul's words and "boast all the more gladly" about your weakness (verse 9)? Why or why not?*

Day 3

Read Psalm 56:1–4. *This psalmist has enemies! In fact, many of the psalms speak of enemies, so it must be a theme worth considering. Who are your enemies? How do they attack you?*

Day 4

Read Ephesians 3:16–17. *What does Paul pray for? How would you restate it in your own words?*

Day 5

Read Ephesians 3:17–19. *What experience of the Love of Christ have you already had?*

Day 6

Read Ephesians 3:20–21. *What does Paul say is true about God? Do you believe this? If so, what helps you to believe it?*

Day 7

Read Ephesians 3:20–21 again. *What do you want to ask of God in light of these two verses?*

Week 13

GOD ALONE

Discover

It's not possible to go through life trusting nothing or no one at all. If we don't trust God to meet our needs, we will put our trust in something or someone else.

For some people, this misplaced trust is in themselves—they strive to be self-reliant. For other people, it's in those around them—they cling to friends, family, or leaders to feel secure. Some individuals turn to addictions like food, alcohol, or other distractions. But the truth is that no amount of self-reliance, human support, or worldly means can compare to God's sovereign care. When we put our trust in Him, we are placing our faith in the One who is infinitely capable of meeting all our needs.

In this week's study, you will explore why trusting in God as your Protector, Provider, and Security is always the best course to take.

1. *When your trust in God is shaky, who or what are you tempted to trust instead?*

2. *What is one instance where you placed your trust in God and felt His calming Spirit? How can you reinforce that memory when you are tempted to trust in other things?*

Experience

Refuse to worry! In this world there will always be something enticing you to worry. That is the nature of a fallen, fractured planet: Things are not as they should be. So the temptation to be anxious is constantly with you, trying to worm its way into your mind. The best defense is *continual communication with Me, richly seasoned with thanksgiving*. Awareness of My Presence fills your mind with Light and Peace, leaving no room for fear. This awareness lifts you up above your circumstances, enabling you to see problems from My perspective. Live close to Me! Together we can keep the wolves of worry at bay.

– From *Jesus Calling*, March 4

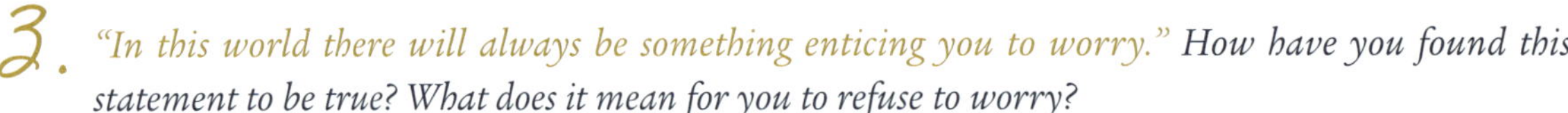

3. *"In this world there will always be something enticing you to worry." How have you found this statement to be true? What does it mean for you to refuse to worry?*

4. *"Awareness of My Presence fills your mind with Light and Peace, leaving no room for fear." What fears do you need the Presence of God to remove from your mind today?*

DWELL

Read 2 Kings 6:8–23. This story from the life of Elisha shows what can happen when you choose to be aware of God's Presence and allow that awareness to "lift you up above your circumstances, enabling you to see problems from [God's] perspective." Even in the face of attacks and desperate circumstances against the Aramean army, Elisha remained calm and steadfast. His unwavering trust in God's power and protection during this "uphill journey" serves as a reminder that God is always in control, no matter what you face.

5. *Where do you notice the themes of blindness and sight repeated in this story?*

6. *How was Elisha able to remain calm in spite of being surrounded by the enemy? What would have happened if he had put his trust in himself?*

7. *What "armies" (challenges, pressures, fears) feel overwhelming to you right now? How will you choose to remain constantly aware of God's Presence in those situations?*

8. *Where in your life do you need to submit your fears to the Lord and see things from His perspective? What "wolves of worry" would you most like to keep at bay?*

Apply

The focus of this week's readings is on trusting in God alone rather than in the many alternatives that people often turn to today. Each day, read the passage slowly, pausing to think about and reflect on what is being said. Remember, this is an opportunity to meet with Jesus and lay all your stresses, struggles, and strains at His feet.

Day 1

Read Isaiah 31:1–3. *In this passage, Isaiah talks to his fellow countrymen who were placing their trust in a military alliance with Egypt. If you were to replace "horses" and "chariots" (verse 1) in this passage with something relevant to your life, what would it be?*

Day 2

Pray through Psalm 20:1–9, stopping with each sentence to ask how it applies to your life. *Write down a few key items that came to mind when you did this.*

Day 3

Read Psalm 49:5–15. *According to the psalmist, in what things* shouldn't *you trust? What reasons does the psalmist offer for not relying on these things?*

Day 4

Reread Psalm 49:15. *The psalmist states that God will redeem his soul "from the power of the grave"* (NKJV). *How does this represent the ultimate reason you should place your trust in the Lord?*

Day 5

Read Psalm 62:1–8. *The psalmist's solution to his problems is to "find rest in God" (verse 5). What do you think this means? How is rest related to trust?*

Day 6

Read Psalm 62:9–10. *The psalmist says social status is meaningless. In what ways has status—how important you are in other people's eyes—motivated you in the past?*

Day 7

Read Psalm 62:11–12. *The psalmist says God is the source of power and unfailing Love. In what areas of your life do you need those things?*

Week 14

DEPENDENT ON GOD

Discover

Life can catch us by surprise. The unexpected loss of a loved one reshapes our entire existence. A job offer (or the loss of a job) redirects our future. And sometimes God calls us to follow Him on an entirely different path.

When your journey takes a different turn than you hoped, how do you respond? Do you cling to worry, questioning God's intentions? Or do you lean on Him more and more for strength and guidance? The truth is that many of us find ourselves caught in between. We are unsure of the way ahead, yet we long to trust in the Lord.

This week's study invites you to reflect on those moments of sudden change and explore what it means to fully rely on God when the unexpected occurs. For the truth is you *can* move forward with faith, trusting the goodness of God's plans even when they differ from your own.

1. *What have been some of the major turning points in your journey—the life-altering ones, positive or negative? List three to five events that stand out to you as the most significant.*

2. *Which, if any, of those major turning points were things you didn't plan? How did you deal with them?*

Experience

I AM LEADING YOU, STEP BY STEP, through your life. Hold My hand in trusting dependence, letting Me guide you through this day. Your future looks uncertain and feels flimsy—even precarious. That is how it should be. *Secret things belong to the Lord*, and future things are secret things. When you try to figure out the future, you are grasping at things that are Mine. This, like all forms of worry, is an act of rebellion: doubting My promises to care for you.

Whenever you find yourself worrying about the future, repent and return to Me. I will show you the next step forward, and the one after that, and the one after that. Relax and enjoy the journey in My Presence, trusting Me to open up the way before you as you go.

– From *Jesus Calling*, February 26

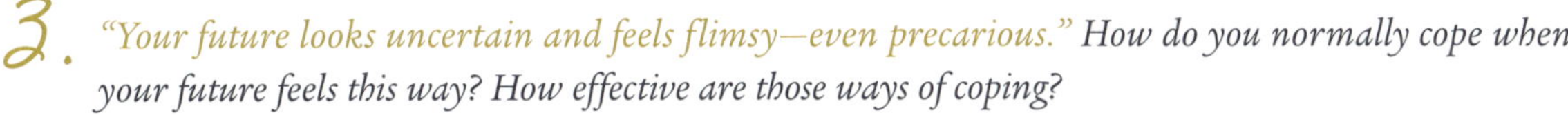

3. *"Your future looks uncertain and feels flimsy—even precarious." How do you normally cope when your future feels this way? How effective are those ways of coping?*

4. *"When you try to figure out the future, you are grasping at things that are Mine." What does this say about how you should deal with your fears about the future? What would it look like in practice for you to truly leave your future in God's hands?*

Dwell

Read Luke 1:26–38. This story reminds us that when God shows us "the next step forward, and the one after that, and the one after that," often those steps will lead to a far different place than we envisioned. In the culture of Mary's day, pregnancy out of wedlock was a cataclysmic disgrace. It could easily have left her an outcast, rejected by her fiancé, family, and village. Yet in spite of this, Mary found peace in surrendering her plans—and herself—into God's hands.

5. *The angel told Mary that she was "highly favored" (verse 28) and the Lord was with her. In spite of this, why do you think Mary was "greatly troubled" (verse 29) at Gabriel's greeting?*

6. *What did the angel reveal about God's plans for Mary? What type of trust on her part would have been required for her to not "try to figure out the future"?*

7. *Even though Gabriel said that Mary was going to become pregnant without the physical involvement of her fiancé—thus opening her to disgrace—she didn't meet the announcement with a catalog of worries. What was Mary's response instead?*

8. *Gabriel emphasized that "with God nothing will be impossible" (verse 37 NKJV). Where in your life do you need to be reminded of that truth? What would it look like for you to let go of your plans and just trust the Lord to "open up the way before you as you go"?*

Apply

The focus of this week's readings is on depending on God during times of change. Each day, read the passage slowly, pausing to think about what is being said. Remember, this is your invitation to reflect on what it means to rely on Christ when the unexpected occurs.

Day 1

Read John 15:5. *Ponder the image of Jesus as the vine and you as a branch of that vine. What does this image tell you about how dependence on Jesus works? Why can you do nothing apart from Him?*

Day 2

Read Colossians 2:6–7. *How would consciously choosing to stay rooted in Jesus help you deal with a time of change? What practices does that involve?*

Day 3

Read Jeremiah 17:5–8. *Why is it disastrous to place your ultimate trust in people or yourself?*

Day 4

Read Isaiah 40:30–31. *Strength comes to those who "wait on" (NKJV) or "hope in" (NIV) the Lord. What does it mean to wait on or hope in God's guidance?*

Day 5

Read Isaiah 40:30–31 again. *What are the benefits of waiting on the Lord? How can you build this into your life even more than you are now?*

Day 6

Read Psalm 32:8–11. *When has God very clearly treated you with unfailing love in the past? Where do you see Him treating you that way now?*

Day 7

Read Proverbs 16:3. *What does it mean to commit your ways to God? Is it a matter of asking Him to bless what you have decided to pursue? Where do trust and dependence fit in?*

Week 15

INTO THE UNKNOWN

Discover

Failure. Nobody enjoys it. In fact, some of us hate it so much that we will avoid trying new things just so we *won't* fail.

However, trusting God often means you will have to step out of the familiar into the unknown. God might even ask you to move forward when a good outcome seems almost impossible. These moments of surrender will push you to completely rely on Him, which is exactly the position you need to be in. Whether your stepping out yields failure or success in the short-term, God is using every step to shape you, grow your faith, and fulfill His purpose in your life over the long-term.

In this week's study, you will explore what it means to take that leap of trust and discover some of the ways God equips you to do so.

1. *Complete this sentence: "My greatest fear in facing the unknown is . . ."*

2. *How have you seen God equip you when you have faced the unknown?*

Experience

You can achieve the victorious life through living in deep dependence on Me. People usually associate victory with success: not falling or stumbling, not making mistakes. But those who are successful in their own strength tend to go their own way, forgetting about Me. It is through problems and failure, weakness and neediness, that you learn to rely on Me.

True dependence is not simply asking Me to bless what you have decided to do. It is coming to Me with an open mind and heart, inviting Me to plant My desires within you. I may infuse within you a dream that seems far beyond your reach. You know that in yourself you cannot achieve such a goal. Thus begins your journey of profound reliance on Me. It is a faith-walk, taken one step at a time, leaning on Me as much as you need. This is not a path of continual success but of multiple failures. However, each failure is followed by a growth spurt, nourished by increased reliance on Me. Enjoy the blessedness of a victorious life, through deepening your dependence on Me.

— From *Jesus Calling*, January 5

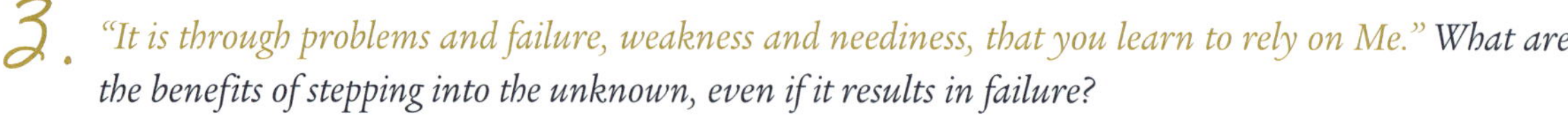

3. *"It is through problems and failure, weakness and neediness, that you learn to rely on Me." What are the benefits of stepping into the unknown, even if it results in failure?*

4. *"I may infuse within you a dream that seems far beyond your reach." Why is it best to ask the Lord to plant His desires in your heart? Why might a person resist doing this?*

Dwell

Read Matthew 14:22–33. Notice the disciples did not initially recognize Jesus amid the chaos of the threatening waves and stormy winds. That revelation was made clear *during* the storm in the midst of their "problems and failure, weakness and neediness." Had the disciples never experienced such a frightening and seemingly uncertain situation, they would have missed out on witnessing God's glory—and the way it strengthened their faith.

5. *It was Jesus who "made the disciples get into the boat" (verse 22) and head across the sea in the midst of a brewing storm. Why do you think He did this? What does this reveal about the types of stormy situations that God might allow to come into your life?*

6. *Jesus immediately identified Himself by saying, "Take courage! It is I. Don't be afraid" (verse 27). How does knowing that Jesus is Present change how you face challenges?*

7. *Peter is the only disciple who was willing to take a "faith-walk." He stepped out of the boat in boldness but sank when he took his focus off Jesus and worried about the wind and the waves. How does this mirror the tension between faith and fear in your life?*

8. *Peter and at least three of the other disciples were seasoned fishermen who were used to seeing storms on the sea. What did they learn about their "weakness and neediness" in this account? What does this story reveal about your need for true dependence on Christ?*

Apply

The focus of this week's readings is on trusting God enough to step into the unknown—whatever outcomes that might bring. Each day, read the passage slowly, pausing to think about what is being said as it relates to trusting God enough to step out of the familiar and into the unknown. Remember, this is your opportunity to personally meet with Jesus.

Day 1

Read Jeremiah 1:4–10. *In this passage, God calls Jeremiah to be a prophet. Why was Jeremiah's youth and inexperience irrelevant? How does this apply to your life and inexperience?*

Day 2

Read Psalm 18:27–29. *Why do you think the Lord favors the humble over the haughty?*

Day 3

Read Psalm 18:27–29 again. *Complete this sentence: "With the Lord I can __________________________." What does God want you to be brave enough to do in complete dependence on Him?*

Day 4

Read Psalm 18:30–36. *What does this passage promise the Lord will do for those who trust in Him? For what battles or unknown situations do you need this kind of help?*

Day 5

Read Isaiah 12:2–6. *Consider each of the things the prophet says the people will proclaim about the Lord. If you were to proclaim to others the things God has done, what would you say?*

Day 6

Read Joshua 2:1–13. *Rahab risked her life to hide spies from the Lord's army. How did fear of the unknown move her toward the Lord rather than away from Him?*

Day 7

Read Joshua 2:1–13 again. *In which area of your life is God asking you to take a risk? How can you move toward the Lord in that situation rather than away from Him?*

Week 16

FOLLOWING AS GOD LEADS

Discover

Not everybody likes to follow. Not being in charge feels passive, and we fear the loss of control. Yet depending on God means trusting in Him in all circumstances, including the ones we think we can handle on our own.

God's purposes are never passive. Following Him calls for a boldness of faith that looks beyond the limited possibilities our eyes can see. Sometimes this involves letting go of our fears, our worries, our complaints—or our pride. Other times, it's about obediently stepping forward to complete the tasks He has placed before us. Either way, dependence on God requires running our ideas and emotions through Him before taking action. In this way, we learn to discern His will and the motives and responses He wants us to have.

In this week's study, you will explore what it means to completely trust in God's control without reservation and faithfully follow His lead.

1. *What is one problem you've had in your life that you can recall purposefully entrusting to God to resolve without fear or worry?*

2. *What did you learn from that experience that helped you trust God more in the future?*

Experience

Come to Me with your plans held in abeyance. *Worship Me in spirit and in truth*, allowing My Glory to permeate your entire being. Trust Me enough to let Me guide you through this day, accomplishing My purposes in My timing. Subordinate your myriad plans to My Master Plan. I am sovereign over every aspect of your life!

The challenge continually before you is to trust Me and search for My way through each day. Do not blindly follow your habitual route, or you will miss what I have prepared for you. *As the heavens are higher than the earth, so are My ways higher than your ways and My thoughts than your thoughts.*

– From *Jesus Calling*, May 18

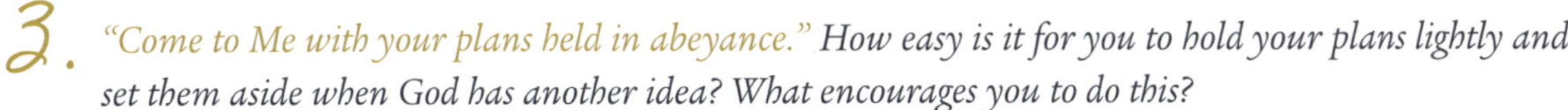

3. *"Come to Me with your plans held in abeyance." How easy is it for you to hold your plans lightly and set them aside when God has another idea? What encourages you to do this?*

4. *"Trust Me and search for My way through each day." What helps you to do this? Do you typically sense God's way or does it tend to be a mystery? Explain your response.*

Dwell

Read Luke 9:10–17. In this scene, Jesus calls upon the tired, emotionally drained disciples to feed a hungry crowd. At first, the disciples are overwhelmed and just want to send everyone away. But Jesus instructs them, "You give them something to eat" (verse 13). In response, the disciples bring a small boy's lunch of five loaves of bread and two fish—which Jesus miraculously multiplies to feed more than five thousand people. From this story we learn, "Do not blindly follow your habitual route, or you will miss what [Christ has] prepared for you."

5. *The "plan" was for Jesus and the disciples to withdraw to a quiet place to get away from the crowds. What happened instead? How did Jesus deal with this change in plans?*

6. *The disciples' "habitual route" (typical way of thinking) was to see things from an earthly perspective—even though the Son of God was with them. How did Jesus challenge that habitual way of thinking? What did He instruct them to do instead?*

7. *When has Jesus asked you to take action in a situation like He did with the disciples in this story? How did you respond? Were you inclined to say, "No, I can't" or perhaps "Yes, I will—in my own strength"? Explain your response.*

8. *How does this miracle illustrate the abundance of God's kingdom (everyone is satisfied and even leftovers are gathered)? What steps will you take this week to trust Jesus with the "little" you have so you can watch and see how He multiplies it?*

Apply

The focus of this week's readings is on relying on God to enable you to do what He has given you to do. Each day, read the passage slowly, pausing to think about what is being said. Remember, this is your opportunity to discover how you can trust in God without reservation.

Day 1

Read Luke 11:5–8. *This story presents an outrageous picture of God. How is God like the friend who has locked up his house and gone to bed? How is He different?*

Day 2

Read Luke 11:5–8 again. *Believers in Christ are encouraged in verse 8 to use "shameless audacity" (NIV) or "persistence" (NKJV) in asking for things from their heavenly Father. How does your current situation call for shameless audacity in prayer?*

Day 3

Read Luke 11:9–10. *What is something you have been asking God to give you for a long time? How do you feel about continuing to ask for it?*

Day 4

Read Luke 11:9–10 again. *How easy is it for you to keep knocking on a door that hasn't yet opened? Why do you think God wants you to continue pursuing Him in your prayers?*

Day 5

Read Luke 11:11–13. *Trust in your heavenly Father might be harder for you to build if you have had an untrustworthy earthly model, but what does this passage say about why you can trust God? Why do you think Jesus also emphasizes praying for the Holy Spirit?*

Day 6

Read Psalm 56:3–4. *As you seek to obey what God has given you to do, do you fear what mortals can do to you? If so, what do you fear? How is God stronger than those things?*

Day 7

Read Habakkuk 3:19. *Write a prayer of willingness to go wherever God leads you. Also express your trust that He will provide you with "deer's feet" to tread there!*

Week 17

STANDING FIRM IN HOPE

Discover

People typically use the word *hope* to express a wish or a desire: "I hope you feel better" or "I'm hoping for a better job." Sometimes they even tie it to positive thinking, as if wishing hard enough can make their desire come true. Yet, ultimately, this kind of hope is rooted in uncertainty because no one can be sure of what will happen in this life.

The hope found in the Bible, however, stands distinct. Instead of mere wishes or optimism, the biblical writers describe unwavering confidence grounded in God Himself, assured by Christ, and sealed by the Holy Spirit. Although many of God's promises are still to come, their rock-solid certainty makes all the difference for those who are waiting on the Lord.

In this week's study, you will unpack the unique nature of biblical hope and discover why it is worth waiting for.

1. *What are three things you long for but don't yet have?*

2. *How confident are you of getting those things? Why?*

Experience

WAITING, TRUSTING, AND HOPING are intricately connected, like golden strands interwoven to form a strong chain. Trusting is the central strand because it is the response from My children that I desire the most. Waiting and hoping embellish the central strand and strengthen the chain that connects you to Me. Waiting for Me to work, with your eyes on Me, is evidence that you really do trust Me. If you mouth the words "I trust You" while anxiously trying to make things go your way, your words ring hollow. Hoping is future-directed, connecting you to your inheritance in heaven. However, the benefits of hope fall fully on you in the present.

Because you are Mine, you don't just pass time in your waiting. You can wait expectantly, in hopeful trust. Keep your "antennae" out to pick up even the faintest glimmer of My Presence.

– From *Jesus Calling*, March 12

3. *"Waiting, trusting, and hoping are intricately connected." Why is it important to treat waiting, trusting, and hoping like strands of a cord that connect you to God?*

4. *"Hoping is future-directed." What does it mean that your hope is future-directed? What are the present benefits—in this life—of possessing such a hope?*

DWELL

Read Romans 8:18–25. In this passage, the apostle Paul exhorts you to hold fast to faith, especially when challenges and hardships arise. Faith points you to God's promises; hope gives you joyful expectation of His fulfilled word. Faith lays the foundation; hope builds on it, urging you to patiently endure trials and delays. When you belong to Christ, "you don't just pass time in your waiting." Rather, you find that "you can wait expectantly, in hopeful trust."

5. *Paul says your present sufferings are "not worth comparing" (verse 18) with the future glory to come. How does that perspective challenge or comfort you right now?*

6. *Paul notes that all of creation itself waits in "eager expectation" (verse 19) for further revelation from the Lord. What do you think he means by this? In what sense is creation waiting to "be liberated from its bondage to decay" (verse 21)?*

7. *Paul writes that "hope that is seen is no hope" and no one "hopes for what they already have" (verse 24). How does that help you to understand what hope actually is?*

8. *How does this passage demonstrate the intricate connection between "waiting, trusting, and hoping"? What hope do you have in the present as you wait for future glory?*

Apply

The focus of this week's readings is on sustaining a hope-filled trust beyond your doubts or circumstances. Each day, read the passage slowly, pausing to reflect on it. Remember, this is an opportunity to meet with Jesus and unpack the unique nature of biblical hope.

Day 1

Read Romans 8:26–27. *Do you ever offer up "wordless groans" when you pray? Explain.*

Day 2

Read Romans 8:26–27 again. *How does the Holy Spirit's activity help you wait with patience? How hard is it for you currently to wait with patience?*

Day 3

Read Romans 8:28–30. *What things in your life have caused you to question whether God is working through them for your good? Pray over this list and ask God the Father to confidently and patiently strengthen your hope as He conforms you to the image of His Son.*

Day 4

Read Lamentations 3:19–23. *List some examples of how the Lord's compassions are new every morning. Take some time to be honest with Him and to thank Him for today's compassions.*

Day 5

Read Lamentations 3:24–25. *How convinced are you that the Lord is good to those whose hope is in Him? What evidence do you have?*

Day 6

Read Lamentations 3:26–29. *Do you trust the Lord enough to sit in silence with a heavy weight on your shoulders if He has put it there? Write a note to Him about this.*

Day 7

Read Lamentations 3:30–33. *Does it help you to know that the Lord doesn't take pleasure in bringing affliction on anyone? If this is true, then why doesn't He use His power to prevent it?*

Week 18

ULTIMATE HOPE

Discover

All too often we attach our hopes to things that are good . . . but not *ultimately* good. We hope for excellent health, children who thrive, a joyful marriage, fulfilling work, or financial security. God, in His kindness, may bless us with those things. However, He offers something far greater to us: a hope that never fails.

Anchoring our hope in Him means we can simultaneously experience His Presence in this life and anticipate the future fulfillment of this hope. Although heaven may feel far off or abstract, the glimpses of it that God has given us through His Word are an invitation to live with an eternal perspective today.

In this week's study, you will step into the throne room of heaven as described in the Bible to gain a clearer vision of the ultimate hope and unshakable confidence you have in God.

1. *Describe your mental picture of heaven. How attractive does it seem to you? How real does it seem?*

2. *What are the things you hope for when you get to heaven?*

Experience

SEEK MY FACE, and you will find all that you have longed for. The deepest yearnings of your heart are for intimacy with Me. I know because I designed you to desire Me. Do not feel guilty about taking time to be still in My Presence. You are simply responding to the tugs of divinity within you. I made you in My image, and I hid heaven in your heart. Your yearning for Me is a form of homesickness: longing for your true home in heaven.

Do not be afraid to be different from other people. The path I have called you to travel is exquisitely right for you. The more closely you follow My leading, the more fully I can develop your gifts. To follow Me wholeheartedly, you must relinquish your desire to please other people. However, your closeness to Me will bless others by enabling you to shine brightly in this dark world.

— From *Jesus Calling*, July 20

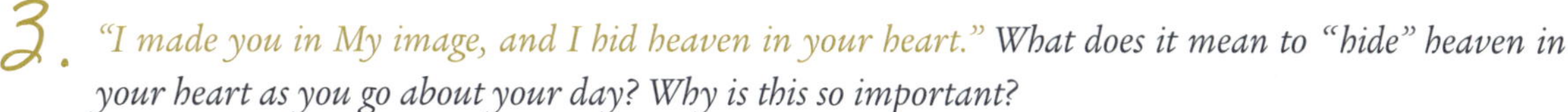

3. *"I made you in My image, and I hid heaven in your heart." What does it mean to "hide" heaven in your heart as you go about your day? Why is this so important?*

4. *"Your yearning for Me is a form of homesickness." How aware are you of your yearning for Jesus and your true home in heaven? To what extent do you yearn more for other things?*

Dwell

Read Revelation 4:2–11 and consider how "your yearning for [Christ] is a form of homesickness: longing for your true home in heaven." In these passages, the apostle John attempts to describe a vision of what heaven is like. As you read, note that the living creatures represent a form of angelic beings and the twenty-four elders symbolize the leaders of God's people (twelve patriarchs of the Old Testament and twelve apostles of the New Testament). The Lamb who was slain is Jesus, who sacrificed His life as an offering on our behalf.

5. *John can't quite describe what the One on the throne looks like. The best he can do is say that He "had the appearance of jasper [a gemstone that comes in a variety of colors] and ruby" (verse 3). What mental picture do you get from John's description of God?*

6. *The four living creatures never stop proclaiming God is "holy, holy, holy" (verse 8). The word* holy *means to be set apart, wholly other, and morally pure. What does this reveal about heaven? What does it reveal about the "tugs of divinity" God has placed in you?*

7. *John writes that whenever the living creatures give glory to God, the twenty-four elders "worship him who lives for ever and ever" (verse 10). Why do you think worship is such a central activity of heaven? What are the implications for believers here and now?*

8. *What is your reaction to this picture of God's Presence? Are you drawn to it with longing, or does it make you want to step back in awe? Explain your response.*

Apply

The focus of this week's readings is on the relevance your future in heaven has on your present. Each day, read the passages slowly, pausing to think about what is being said. Remember, this is an opportunity to meet with Jesus and consider the ultimate hope you have in Him.

Day 1

Read 1 Peter 1:3–5. *What is the reason for your living hope? What do you hope for?*

Day 2

Read 1 Peter 1:6–7. *Peter begins by saying, "In all this you greatly rejoice," referring to what he mentioned in verses 3–5. How greatly do you rejoice in Jesus' resurrection? Why?*

Day 3

Read 1 Peter 1:6–7 again. *What reasons for present trials does Peter provide? Do his words encourage you to have joy despite your trials? Explain your response.*

Day 4

Read 1 Peter 1:8–9. *How would you describe your feelings about the salvation of your soul? What impact does the perspective of this passage have on you?*

Day 5

Read Hebrews 6:10–11. *What does the author want believers in Christ to do while they wait for their hope to be fully realized?*

Day 6

Read Hebrews 6:12. *Does busyness with other things tend to crowd out your time to devote to growth in love? If so, what might be the consequences?*

Day 7

Read Hebrews 6:19. *How is biblical hope a sure and steadfast anchor for the soul? How can you better anchor yourself in God and the hope of eternal life with Him?*

Week 19

NEVER FAR AWAY

Discover

Worship is not only central to God's eternal plan but also gives each of us as believers in Christ a foretaste of the joy—and never-ending hope—of heaven. Our earthly circumstances may be at a crisis point, or all may be well. Regardless, in *every* circumstance, praising and glorifying God enriches our lives and reinforces the reality of His promises.

While heaven is a place filled with worship, the Bible also portrays it as the setting of a grand banquet—a celebration of fellowship and abundance. In the promise of these eternal celebrations, God continually encourages us as we journey here on earth, reminding us that the joy of heaven is never far away. It can be ours, even in the darkest times.

In this week's study, you will discover more about that glorious future and the encouragement it holds for you today.

1. *When you were a child, what special meals did you have at family celebrations? Give a few examples.*

2. *As an adult, what special things do you do with your family to celebrate your time together? Give a few examples.*

Experience

You are My beloved child. *I chose you before the foundation of the world*, to walk with Me along paths designed uniquely for you. Concentrate on keeping in step with Me instead of trying to anticipate My plans for you. If you trust that My plans are *to prosper you and not to harm you*, you can relax and enjoy the present moment.

Your hope and your future are rooted in heaven, where eternal ecstasy awaits you. Nothing can rob you of your inheritance of unimaginable riches and well-being. Sometimes I grant you glimpses of your glorious future, to encourage you and spur you on. But your main focus should be staying close to Me. I set the pace in keeping with your needs and My purposes.

– From *Jesus Calling*, June 18

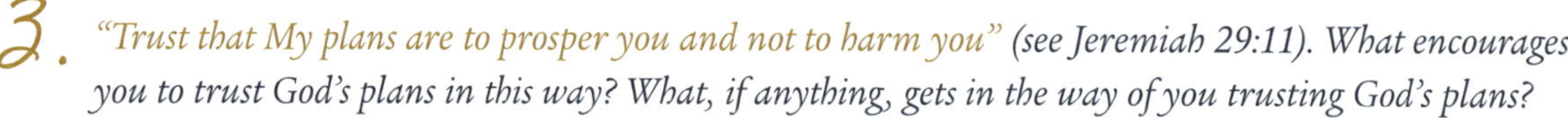

3. *"Trust that My plans are to prosper you and not to harm you" (see Jeremiah 29:11). What encourages you to trust God's plans in this way? What, if anything, gets in the way of you trusting God's plans?*

4. *"Your main focus should be staying close to Me." How has God encouraged you by showing you glimpses of your glorious future? How do you nurture closeness with Him?*

Dwell

Read Isaiah 25:6–9. Sometimes God will "grant you glimpses of your glorious future, to encourage you and spur you on." This is what God does in this passage. He gives the prophet Isaiah a vision of the final destiny of the mountaintop city of Jerusalem, where he lived. The city was presently filled with problems, but God revealed that one day a heavenly Jerusalem would fulfill the city's true purpose. This heavenly Jerusalem is every Christian's destiny!

5. *Imagine a banquet filled with "rich food" and "aged wine" (verse 6) inside the most glorious city you've ever seen. What is God saying about heaven when He describes it in these terms? What might the rich food and aged wine symbolize about heaven?*

6. *God says the heavenly banquet will be for all peoples. Picture a celebratory feast with people from all parts of the world. Why are the guests an important part of the occasion? Who are some of the people you look forward to seeing at this banquet?*

7. *God says He will "swallow up death forever" (verse 8). It will no longer be like a shroud that covers whole nations. What does this say about God's ultimate plans for His people? What do you envision when you picture an eternity where death does not exist?*

8. *Praise of the host will be part of the banquet celebration. Why do you think the people repeat the phrase "we trusted in him" (verse 9) when they consider what God has done? What role should trust in God play in your preparation for this hoped-for banquet?*

Apply

The focus of this week's readings is on the here-and-now implications of the future heavenly banquet. Each day this week, read the passage slowly, pausing to think about what is being said. Remember, this is your opportunity to reflect on the glorious future God has for you.

Day 1

Read Luke 14:15–20. *What excuses do people make today for declining God's invitation to join Him at the celebration feast in heaven? What excuses have you struggled with regarding accepting this invitation? Why do these excuses often seem so convincing?*

Day 2

Read Luke 14:21–24. *How does the master hosting the banquet deal with the excuses? How does your invitation to the banquet make you feel?*

Day 3

Read Psalm 36:7–9. *When the psalmist says, "They feast on the abundance of your house" (verse 8), what does he mean? What is the abundance God provides?*

Day 4

Read 2 Corinthians 9:8. *Are you feasting? Do you experience abundance "for every good work" (NKJV) or does your life feel more like scarcity? Explain.*

Day 5

Read John 6:27–29. *What does it mean to believe in Jesus? What does this involve besides believing information about Him?*

Day 6

Read John 6:35. *What does Jesus mean in calling Himself the "bread of life"? Do you tend to be more focused on your physical needs or your spiritual needs? Why is that the case?*

Day 7

Read John 6:48–52. *Why did Jesus place so much emphasis on the need for spiritual food?*

Week 20

BLESSED ASSURANCE

Discover

When life in this world is weighing us down with seemingly endless sorrows, it's natural to wonder if the darkness will ever lift. Yet the promises of God remain, like the shining of the sun above the storm clouds, assuring us that the pains of earth will not last.

To our blessing and relief, God has determined that a day is coming when every tear will be wiped away. Even now, His Presence is with us—filling us with hope and renewing our strength for each day.

In this week's study, you will immerse yourself in God's promised vision of the future as recorded in the book of Revelation. This future of unimaginable joy and peace will empower you to endure your current trials with faith and perseverance.

1. *List three recent trials you have faced that have put your hope in God to the test.*

2. *What did those situations teach you?*

Experience

HEAVEN IS both present and future. As you walk along your life-path holding My hand, you are already in touch with the essence of heaven: nearness to Me. You can also find many hints of heaven along your pathway because the earth is radiantly alive with My Presence. Shimmering sunshine awakens your heart, gently reminding you of My brilliant Light. Birds and flowers, trees and skies evoke praises to My holy Name. Keep your eyes and ears fully open as you journey with Me.

At the end of your life-path is an entrance to heaven. Only I know when you will reach that destination, but I am preparing you for it each step of the way. The absolute certainty of your heavenly home gives you Peace and Joy, to help you along your journey. You know that you will reach your home in My perfect timing: not one moment too soon or too late. Let the hope of heaven encourage you, as you walk along the path of Life with Me.

– From *Jesus Calling*, April 14

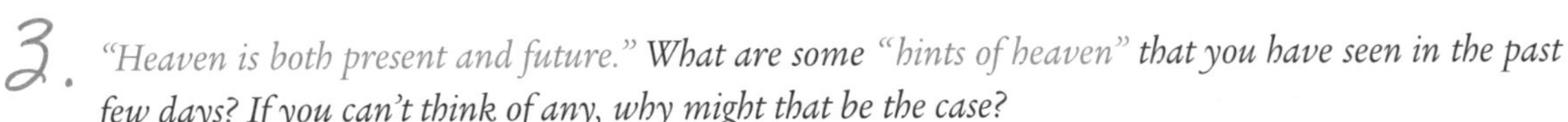

3. *"Heaven is both present and future." What are some "hints of heaven" that you have seen in the past few days? If you can't think of any, why might that be the case?*

4. *"Walk along your life-path holding My hand." What does it mean, in practical terms, for you to journey through this life holding Jesus' hand? How are you able to do that?*

Dwell

Read Revelation 21:1–5, 9–12, 18–27. John's vision of the heavenly Jerusalem—safe, beautiful, and filled with life—descending to a renewed earth is a reminder of the eternity all believers share. God desires this "hope of heaven [to] encourage you, as you walk along the path of Life with [Him]." For John, who lived in a time when the wilderness represented danger and the countryside represented toil, the vision was an assurance of peace and restoration.

5. *What are your overall impressions of the New Jerusalem when you read these passages? What hints of this picture of your eternal home do you find on this earth?*

6. *John writes that God will dwell in the midst of His people in the new Jerusalem, with no distance between them. Why is this significant?*

7. *In what ways is the nearness you can have with God now a picture of the nearness you will have with Him in eternity? How should that impact your life in the present?*

8. *John writes that "those whose names are written in the Lamb's book of life" (verse 27) have absolute certainty of this vision of their heavenly home (see also 1 Peter 1:3–5). How should that certainty give you Peace and Joy and influence the way you handle trials and suffering in this life?*

Apply

The focus of this week's readings is on connecting your eternal hope with your daily life. Each day, read the passage slowly, pausing to think about what is being said. Remember, this is your opportunity to meet with Jesus and consider where you place your hope.

Day 1

Read Ephesians 1:15–18. *What thoughts and feelings do you have about your hope in Christ? How does godly hope influence the way you deal with current circumstances?*

Day 2

Read Ephesians 1:19–23. *Which powers and authorities currently impact your life the most? Do you believe Jesus is far above those? Why or why not?*

Day 3

Read 1 Timothy 6:17–18. *What are the signs that you have put your hope in wealth? Why is it foolish to invest your hope there? How can you be rich in good deeds?*

Day 4

Read 1 Timothy 6:19. *What is "the life that is truly life"? What other kinds of life do people run after that aren't truly life?*

Day 5

Read Hebrews 10:22–25. *How much daily assurance does your faith provide? To what extent do you struggle with doubts? Explain your response.*

Day 6

Read Psalm 25:1–3. *What does it mean to be put to shame? Why are you safe from shame if you hope in God? Are you able to trust that promise? Why or why not?*

Day 7

Read Psalm 25:4–5. *Has there been a time when you have truly put your hope in God all day long? If so, what difference did that make? How would this practice make a difference in your life right now?*

Week 21

HOPE IN A DRY LAND

DISCOVER

Picture the desert, where the sun scorches, the wind stings, and the dryness in the air permeates every breath. Minus shade, shelter, or water, the excruciating conditions of the desert can prove fatal for a person in a matter of hours or days.

For the biblical writers, the desert was more than a physical place—it symbolized deprivation, desperation, severe hardship, and total dependence on the Lord. When God, through prophets such as Isaiah, promised to transform the harsh desert into a thriving, prosperous land for His people, it gave them hope. This promise was a declaration of God's power to bring renewal and life where none seemed possible.

In this week's study, you will explore what that promise means for you today. You will also look at how the protection this hope of God's future transformation provides can help you during your driest and most barren seasons.

1. *When you think of the desert, what images or memories come to mind?*

2. *When you think of God's protection, what images or memories come to mind?*

Experience

REMEMBER THAT YOU LIVE IN a fallen world: an abnormal world tainted by sin. Much frustration and failure result from your seeking perfection in this life. There is nothing perfect in this world except Me. That is why closeness to Me satisfies deep yearnings and fills you with Joy.

I have planted longing for perfection in every human heart. This is a good desire, which I alone can fulfill. But most people seek this fulfillment in other people and earthly pleasures or achievements. Thus they create idols, before which they bow down. *I will have no other gods before Me!* Make Me the deepest desire of your heart. Let Me fulfill your yearning for perfection.

– From *Jesus Calling*, June 5

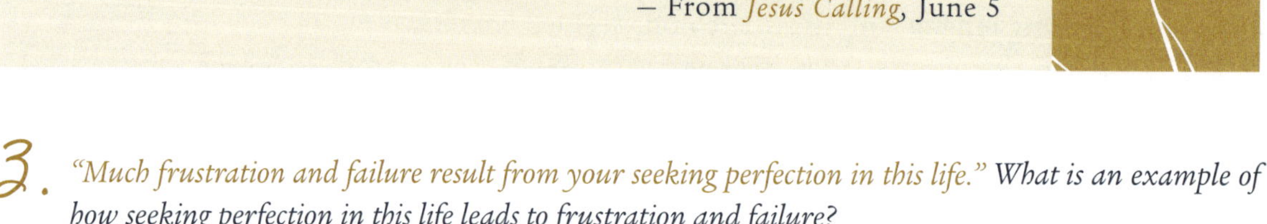

3. *"Much frustration and failure result from your seeking perfection in this life." What is an example of how seeking perfection in this life leads to frustration and failure?*

4. *"Make Me the deepest desire of your heart." What are some desires in your heart that might be getting in the way of you making Jesus the* deepest *desire of your heart?*

Dwell

Read Isaiah 35:1–2, 5–10. As you know only too well, "you live in a fallen world: an abnormal world tainted by sin." However, in these passages, the prophet Isaiah paints a beautiful picture of the transformation and restoration that will come when Christ returns. He describes a once dangerous desert blossoming into a fertile and vibrant land. Isaiah's words remind us that God's promises are sure, bringing forth life where none was thought possible.

5. *The "desert" and "parched land" (verse 1) represent the desolation that comes from living "in a fallen world" that is "tainted by sin." Given this, what is the prophet Isaiah expressing when he says the desert will "rejoice greatly" and "shout for joy" (verse 2)?*

6. *Not only will "the desert and the parched land" (verse 1) be transformed but so also will be the people (the blind, the lame, the deaf). What transformations in this fallen world, or in individual lives, do you most look forward to seeing? Why those transformations?*

7. *Isaiah wrote that "a highway will be there" called "the Way of Holiness" (verse 8). What does this highway represent? Who will be able to traverse that highway?*

8. *The picture that Isaiah paints is of a world that has been restored at the return of Jesus and is now perfect. How do you respond when you read what this world will be like? What does this say about how God has "planted longing for perfection" in your heart?*

Apply

The focus of this week's readings is on the hope you have as recorded in the book of Isaiah. Each day, read the passage slowly, pausing to think about what is being said. Remember, this is your opportunity to explore God's promise to bring renewal to your life.

Day 1

Read Isaiah 35:3–4. *What hope do you gain from Isaiah's vision?*

Day 2

Read Isaiah 35:3–4 again. *Does it help you to know that God will come to save you eventually, even if that is years from now? Explain your response.*

Day 3

Read Isaiah 11:3–5. *These words refer to Jesus when He comes as King to rule. What can you expect Him to do? What longings does the return of Christ stir in you?*

Day 4

Read Isaiah 11:6–9. *In light of these words about Christ's future kingdom, where would you like to see the knowledge of the Lord spread today?*

Day 5

Read Isaiah 32:1–5. *How easy is it for you to imagine rulers who are like "a shelter from the wind" (verse 2)? What would make them that way? If you live in peace and safety, offer God a prayer of thanks for that fact.*

Day 6

Read Isaiah 49:14–16. *Are you ever tempted to think that the Lord has forsaken you? What assurances does this passage give if you feel that way? How do these assurances affect you?*

Day 7

Read John 20:24–29. *Think about the wounds on the palms of Jesus' hands from being nailed to the cross. How is that like having your name engraved on His hands?*

Week 22

HOPE OF RESURRECTION

Discover

Among the religions that teach immortality, Christianity offers a distinct and singularly true vision. Just as Jesus was bodily raised from the dead into a glorified form, so all those who have put their faith in Him will one day experience a resurrection. Our souls will be clothed in renewed bodies that are uniquely our own.

This is not reincarnation, where mortal bodies return to live another life in another state in a broken world. Rather, our resurrection will be a one-time event, occurring when heaven and earth are made new. As faithful followers of Christ, we will receive glorified bodies suited for inhabiting a restored, perfect creation! Such an all-encompassing promise of renewal is deeply physical, deeply personal, and deeply rooted in God's transforming power.

In this week's study, you will explore the profound implications of this great hope and how you should live in light of this coming renewal.

1. *It's easy to think of things you don't like about your body because it is imperfect now. So instead, what are three things about your body you're grateful for?*

2. *How would you describe your thoughts and feelings of one day not having a body that is marred by physical ailments?*

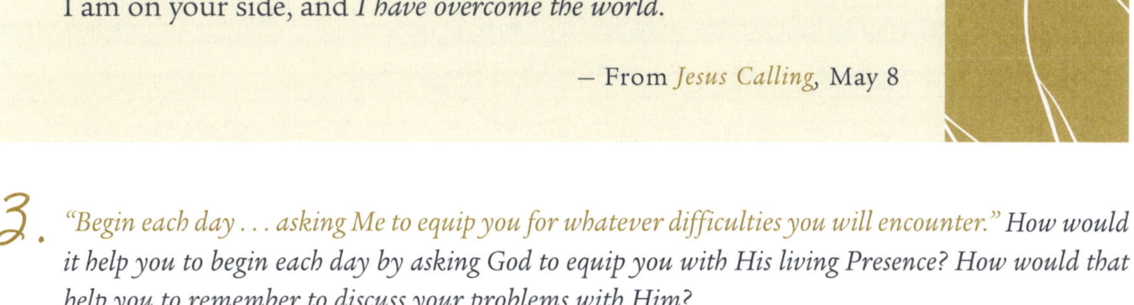

Experience

Do not long for the absence of problems in your life. That is an unrealistic goal since *in this world you will have trouble*. You have an eternity of problem-free living reserved for you in heaven. Rejoice in that inheritance, which no one can take away from you, but do not seek your heaven on earth.

Begin each day anticipating problems, asking Me to equip you for whatever difficulties you will encounter. The best equipping is My living Presence, *My hand that never lets go of yours*. Discuss everything with Me. Take a lighthearted view of trouble, seeing it as a challenge that you and I together can handle. Remember that I am on your side, and *I have overcome the world.*

– From *Jesus Calling*, May 8

3. *"Begin each day . . . asking Me to equip you for whatever difficulties you will encounter." How would it help you to begin each day by asking God to equip you with His living Presence? How would that help you to remember to discuss your problems with Him?*

4. *"Take a lighthearted view of trouble, seeing it as a challenge that you and I together can handle." How easy or difficult is it for you to view your troubles in this way? What helps you to be aware that God is on your side when you face troubles?*

DWELL

Read 1 Corinthians 15:35, 42–44, 50–54. The early Christians knew they had an "eternity of problem-free living" reserved for them and an "inheritance, which no one could take away from [them]." Many of them believed this enough to become martyrs! But given this reality that their faith in Jesus could lead to their deaths, they wanted to know the future inheritance in store for them was better than what they were ready to sacrifice on earth. In response, Paul wrote to them about the bodily resurrection of Christians who have died as well as the bodily transformation of those who have not yet died when Jesus returns for His people.

5. *Consider the two kinds of bodies—the "natural" and the "spiritual" that Paul describes in this passage. What are the main differences between these two types of bodies?*

6. *Why does Paul emphasize that the body you will have is imperishable? Why is this important in understanding the type of "problem-free" body you will have in eternity?*

7. *Paul states that death itself will be defeated. How should the reality of Jesus' victory over death relieve you from the fear of death that impacts so many people in the world?*

8. *How could Paul's words help you to "take a lighthearted view of trouble" in this world? What cause does it give you to rejoice when you consider the inheritance you will receive?*

Apply

The focus of this week's readings is on the impact of resurrection hope. Each day, read the passage slowly, pausing to think about what is being said, especially as it relates to your coming resurrected body. Remember, this is an opportunity to meet with Jesus.

Day 1

Read Philippians 3:20–21. *What does it mean for believers here on earth to have their citizenship in heaven?*

Day 2

Read Luke 24:36–43. *Why should followers of Jesus feel joy and amazement at the hope of one day receiving a resurrected body?*

Day 3

Read John 20:19–23. *Why do you think Jesus twice stated the greeting "Peace be with you!" (verses 19, 21)? How can this statement provide you hope in times of despair?*

Day 4

Read John 20:24–29. *Why do you think Jesus still had the wounds from the crucifixion in His hands and His side? Why didn't those go away when He was raised from the dead? Which scars might you be pleased to retain when you receive your resurrection body?*

Day 5

Read 1 Corinthians 15:17–19. *Why does Jesus' resurrection—not just His crucifixion—matter for your salvation?*

Day 6

Read 1 Corinthians 15:55–57. *What did Paul mean when he said that "the sting of death is sin" (verse 56)? Why is sin no longer a deadly danger if you trust in Christ?*

Day 7

Read 1 Corinthians 15:58. *Paul wants your freedom from fear to liberate you to do the Lord's work. Do you feel that liberation? What other related fears still cling to you?*

Week 23

THE EXERCISE OF FAITH

Discover

Imagine a baseball game where the team on the field has a pitcher who only throws slow and easily hittable pitches and no players cover any bases or the outfield. How engaging would that be to watch? The batters would easily score, leaving little room for suspense. If the other team knew their opponent was so weak, they likely wouldn't even bother practicing.

Now think about the "game" of life. Easy victories don't strengthen us or deepen our faith. Rather, our faith grows in those times when we must persevere, trusting in God's plan even when the odds seem stacked against us. The victories that inspire us most—and bring glory to God—are the ones that require courage, persistence, and reliance on His strength.

In this week's study, you will explore how God uses persevering faith to exercise your hope muscles and give you victories worth celebrating.

1. *When you were a child, did you tend to stick to activities you knew you were good at or did you try things that required a lot of effort and the risk of failure? Give an example.*

2. *As an adult, do you try things that require a lot of effort and include the risk of failure? Why might you have been more adventurous as a child than you are now as an adult?*

Experience

Give up the illusion that you deserve a problem-free life. Part of you is still hungering for the resolution of all difficulties. This is a false hope! As I told My disciples, *in the world you will have trouble.* Link your hope not to problem solving in this life but to the promise of an eternity of problem-free life in heaven. Instead of seeking perfection in this fallen world, pour your energy into seeking Me: the Perfect One.

It is possible to enjoy Me and glorify Me in the midst of adverse circumstances. In fact, My Light shines most brightly through believers who trust Me in the dark. That kind of trust is supernatural: a production of My indwelling Spirit. When things seem all wrong, trust Me anyway. I am much less interested in right circumstances than in right responses to whatever comes your way.

— From *Jesus Calling*, January 26

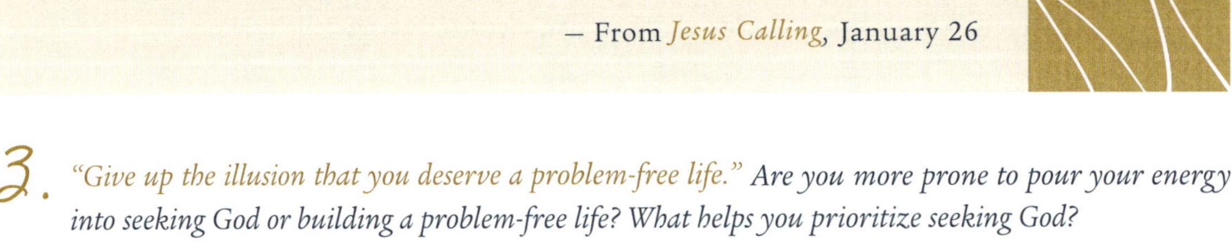

3. *"Give up the illusion that you deserve a problem-free life." Are you more prone to pour your energy into seeking God or building a problem-free life? What helps you prioritize seeking God?*

4. *"Trust Me in the dark." You don't need to give up hope of seeing your difficulties resolved. It's more a matter of holding those hopes lightly so you don't fall into despair when difficulty persists. Is despair ever a temptation for you? If so, what do you do in those situations?*

Dwell

Read Romans 5:1–5. When we are in the midst of trials and suffering, it can be hard for us to see how "[Christ's] Light shines most brightly through believers who trust [Him] in the dark." We might be tempted to give up when challenges come our way, but doing so only leads to despair and a sense of hopeless finality. The choice to persevere, on the other hand, invites God's Presence into our struggles, which means we can trust that our failures are not final. By leaning on His strength and expecting His goodness to prevail, our perspective shifts.

5. *The "hope of the glory of God" (verse 2) is the hope you have of seeing God's magnificent, light-filled Presence face to Face. Why can you "boast" about this hope?*

6. *It is a false hope to believe that you can have "a problem-free life" or live with "the resolution of all difficulties." Instead, Paul writes, you can "glory in [your] sufferings" (verse 3). Why can you do this? What does Paul say suffering produces in your life?*

7. *Suffering doesn't automatically produce perseverance—it can produce bitterness and despair. However, suffering plus God's grace plus your willing cooperation produces perseverance. What attitudes and actions reflect a willingness to cooperate with God?*

8. *Surprisingly, hope doesn't grow where there is an absence of trials or suffering. It needs both the heat and the storms of life in order to blossom. What is it about perseverance that fosters the kind of character that leads to hope?*

Apply

The focus of this week's readings is on perseverance. Each day, read the passage slowly, pausing to think about what is being said. Remember, this is an opportunity to meet with Jesus.

Day 1

Read Titus 2:11. *What did Paul mean when he said, "The grace of God has appeared"? What should be your response to this grace?*

Day 2

Read Titus 2:12–14. *What is your "blessed hope" (verse 13)? Why is doing good an appropriate response to that hope? How does doing good require perseverance?*

Day 3

Read 2 Thessalonians 1:4–10. *Paul wrote these words to a group of believers who were being persecuted for their faith. Why does he boast about them? How does their perseverance prove that God's judgment is right?*

Day 4

Read Hebrews 2:10–11. *While the truth this passage provides doesn't make the bad things you suffer any less bad, it does mean God can bring something good (your holiness) out of them. Do you want holiness enough to endure what you are currently enduring? Why or why not?*

Day 5

Read Hebrews 2:17–18. *What was Jesus' experience with hope? How can His experience strengthen your hope?*

Day 6

Read Hebrews 12:1. *What are the things that hinder you from persevering with hope? How did Jesus demonstrate perseverance?*

Day 7

Read Hebrews 12:2–3. *How can you go about fixing your eyes on Jesus instead of those things that tend to hinder you from persevering with hope?*

Week 24

STRENGTHENED IN HOPE

Discover

As followers of Christ, we carry a steadfast hope in the promise of a glorious future. One day we will see God face-to-Face. We will worship Him alongside the angels, and we will feast at His banquet in eternal joy. Until then, we are called to nurture this hope by seeking His Presence, prioritizing worship, and choosing perseverance over defeat when challenges arise.

Faith undergirds it all. When life gets overwhelming, we draw strength from God, who promises to sustain and renew us as we place our hope in Him. Endurance fueled by faith enables us to trust that, in everyday situations as well as times of trouble, His faithfulness will see us through.

In this week's study, you will explore God's promise to strengthen everyone whose hope remains in Him.

1. *What is one specific thing God has revealed to you recently about receiving Christ's hope?*

2. *How are you grateful for that revelation?*

Experience

I AM THE CULMINATION of all your hopes and desires. *I am the Alpha and the Omega, the first and the last: who is and was and is to come.* Before you knew Me, you expressed your longing for Me in hurtful ways. You were ever so vulnerable to the evil around you in the world. But now My Presence safely shields you, enfolding you in My loving arms. *I have lifted you out of darkness into My marvelous Light.*

Though I have brought many pleasures into your life, not one of them is essential. Receive My blessings with open hands. Enjoy My good gifts, but do not cling to them. Turn your attention to *the Giver of all good things*, and rest in the knowledge that you are complete in Me. The one thing you absolutely need is the one thing you can never lose: My Presence with you.

– From *Jesus Calling*, October 11

3. *"I am the culmination of all your hopes and desires." Think of one of the biggest hopes you have. How is God the culmination of that hope?*

4. *"Enjoy My good gifts, but do not cling to them." Why does God instruct you to receive His blessings with open hands? What happens when you cling to those good gifts?*

Dwell

Read Isaiah 40:27–31. In these verses, the prophet Isaiah addresses the people of Israel (also called Jacob) who were suffering under the difficult circumstances of being exiled from the promised land. The people were falling into doubt and despair, so God sent Isaiah to tell them, "He gives strength to the weary and increases the power of the weak" (verse 29). These words likewise apply to us whenever we are going through adversity.

5. *The people of Israel had been "ever so vulnerable to the evil around [them] in the world"—which had led to their exile. Now, in their captivity, they were complaining, "My cause is disregarded by my God" (verse 27). How did Isaiah argue against that complaint?*

6. *God wanted His people to know that He would never "grow tired or weary" (verse 28) of enfolding them in His loving arms. In dealing with your circumstances, what does it mean to you to know the Lord will never lose sight of you or "grow tired" of helping you?*

7. *Have you ever experienced the strength to "soar on wings like eagles" (verse 31) that Isaiah describes when you put your hope in the Lord? If so, describe your experience.*

8. *God's message to His people was to turn their attention to Him—"the Giver of all good things"—rather than focus on their present circumstances. How does that same message apply to you today? In what area of your life do you need to turn your attention to Him?*

Apply

The focus of this week's readings is on cultivating hope in the Lord. Each day, read the passage slowly, pausing to think about what is being said. Remember, this is your opportunity to meet with Christ and explore God's promise in Scripture to strengthen and sustain you.

Day 1

Read Psalm 62:5. *Why shouldn't you seek your ultimate rest in anything but God? How will other things disappoint you?*

Day 2

Read Psalm 62:6–8. *How does the psalmist describe God? What does it mean to call Him "my rock" (verse 6)?*

Day 3

Read Psalm 43:3–5. *What should be your attitude as you approach the altar of God? What will putting your hope in Him today involve?*

Day 4

Read Psalm 33:16–22. *What are some of the things people are tempted to place their hope in when they fear catastrophes such as war or hunger? Where are you tempted to place your hope when you are fearful?*

Day 5

Read Psalm 33:18 again. *The psalmist says the Lord's caring eyes are on those whose hope is in His "unfailing love." Why should you be confident His Love is unfailing?*

Day 6

Read Psalm 147:10–14. *What pleases the Lord? What are some of the good things He does for those who hope in Him? How has God protected you and satisfied you?*

Day 7

Read Psalm 130:5–8. *What reasons does the psalmist give for putting your hope in the Lord? Do those reasons motivate you? Why or why not? What motivates you the most?*

Week 25

REJOICING ALWAYS

Discover

What role does rejoicing have in your life? Is it mostly reserved for those occasional outbursts of "Praise the Lord!" when you receive good news or an answer to prayer?

Biblically speaking, rejoicing is so much more than just an emotional response; it's meant to be a continual, intentional act of worship. God calls you to worship Him not just formally at church each week but in every setting: at home, at work, when you're alone, and when you're with others. The more you attune your heart to Him, the more rejoicing becomes a natural—and integral—part of your daily life, filling ordinary days with extraordinary grace.

This week, you will explore what rejoicing means, what it does for your spirit, and how you can make it a beautiful, habitual part of your life, just as the Lord intended.

1. *When you were growing up, what role (if any) did rejoicing in God play in your family?*

2. *What impact do you think that might have had on you as an adult?*

Experience

Rejoice in Me always! No matter what is going on, you can rejoice in your Love-relationship with Me. This is *the secret of being content in all circumstances.* So many people dream of the day when they will finally be happy: when they are out of debt, when their children are out of trouble, when they have more leisure time, and so on. While they daydream, their moments are trickling into the ground like precious balm spilling wastefully from overturned bottles.

Fantasizing about future happiness will never bring fulfillment, because fantasy is unreality. Even though I am invisible, I am far more Real than the world you see around you. My reality is eternal and unchanging. Bring your moments to Me, and I will fill them with vibrant Joy. *Now* is the time to rejoice in My Presence!

– From *Jesus Calling*, September 11

3. *"Rejoice in Me always!" What reasons do you have for rejoicing today? What reasons can you name for rejoicing in God always—even when things are not going your way?*

4. *"Bring your moments to Me, and I will fill them with vibrant Joy." What are some moments you can bring to Jesus today and ask Him to fill with His vibrant joy?*

Dwell

Read Philippians 4:4–9. In this passage, the apostle Paul—writing from the confines of prison—offers words of wisdom and encouragement to believers in the city of Philippi. In spite of their trials, such as facing discrimination and persecution because of their faith, they could choose to "rejoice in the Lord always" (verse 4). This wasn't merely a suggestion; it was an invitation to worship. In the same way, "no matter what is going on, you can rejoice in your Love-relationship with [Christ]," knowing "this is the secret of being content in all circumstances."

5. *What does it mean to "rejoice in the Lord always" (verse 4)? How is that different from just positive thinking or willing yourself to have an upbeat mood?*

6. *Paul was not being naïve when he instructed the Philippian believers to "not be anxious about anything" (verse 6). Rather, what were they to do with those anxious moments?*

7. *No matter what is going in your life, "you can rejoice in your Love-relationship with [Christ]." What does Paul say happens when you do this? Why is this more effective than worry?*

8. *What does Paul say you should set your mind on instead of worries? What happens to your mindset and outlook on life when you choose to focus on these things?*

Apply

The theme of this week's readings is rejoicing as a powerful and intentional act of worship. Each day, read the passage slowly, pausing to reflect on what is being said. Remember, this is an opportunity to discover how to rejoice in the Lord always in spite of your trials.

Day 1

Read Habakkuk 3:16–18. *How was it possible for Habakkuk to rejoice in the Lord given the circumstances that he and the people of his nation were facing?*

Day 2

Read Habakkuk 3:17–18 again. *How easy is it for you to have Habakkuk's attitude? What, if anything, gets in the way of you saying, "I will be joyful in God my Savior" (verse 18)?*

Day 3

Read 1 Thessalonians 5:16–18. *Notice the connection between rejoicing, praying continually, and giving thanks. How do they interact? Why is their interconnection so important?*

Day 4

Read Psalm 5:11–12. *What protective blessings has God given you? How is He protecting you?*

Day 5

Read Psalm 13:1–4. *David asked a number of questions of God about his current situation. What questions do you have for God right now? What are your needs?*

Day 6

Read Psalm 13:5–6. *How easy or difficult is it for you to say, "I trust in [God's] unfailing love" (verse 5)? What especially makes it hard for you to express this to the Lord?*

Day 7

Read Psalm 16:5–11. *Why does the psalmist rejoice? Can you rejoice for the same reasons?*

Week 26

CULTIVATING GRATITUDE

Discover

Have you ever witnessed firsthand how a life that is seeded with gratitude can flourish in any situation? Perhaps this describes someone you know. Maybe this describes you! Cultivating thanksgiving—beginning with gratitude for your salvation and becoming a new creation in Christ—enables your heart to freely worship and bear fruit even in difficult seasons.

The more you sow seeds of gratitude, the stronger and deeper your relationship with God grows. While life's challenges may still feel overwhelming at times, you come to recognize that you're not bound by your circumstances. You find that the Lord has provided numerous ways for you to root your mind in His goodness and foster a spirit of thankfulness.

In this week's study, you will explore reasons to give thanks in every situation and the incredible blessings that flow from a grateful heart.

1. *On a scale of 1 to 10, how thankful would you say you are on a daily basis? Why did you give yourself this particular rating?*

2. *What are three things you are thankful for? How quickly did those three things come to mind?*

Experience

A THANKFUL ATTITUDE opens windows of heaven. Spiritual blessings fall freely onto you through those openings into eternity. Moreover, as you look up with a grateful heart, you get glimpses of Glory through those windows. You cannot yet live in heaven, but you can experience foretastes of your ultimate home. Such samples of heavenly fare revive your hope. Thankfulness opens you up to these experiences, which then provide further reasons to be grateful. Thus your path becomes an upward spiral: ever increasing in gladness.

Thankfulness is not some sort of magic formula; it is the language of Love, which enables you to communicate intimately with Me. A thankful mindset does not entail a denial of reality with its plethora of problems. Instead, it *rejoices in Me, your Savior*, in the midst of trials and tribulations. *I am your refuge and strength, an ever-present and well-proved help in trouble.*

– From *Jesus Calling*, November 22

3. *"A thankful attitude opens windows of heaven." What are some of the benefits of thankfulness mentioned in this reading? How have you experienced them?*

4. *"Thankfulness is not some sort of magic formula." What is the difference between being thankful in spite of your circumstances and denying that you have any problems?*

Dwell

Read Luke 17:11–19. This story reveals the importance of having "a thankful attitude" toward Christ. Note that Jesus was traveling near the border of Samaria and Galilee, a region where the Jews and Samaritans lived in close proximity. The Samaritans practiced a religion that was part Jewish and part pagan, and the Jews regarded them as ethnic and religious half-breeds. Relations between the two groups were often hostile. *Leprosy* refers to a number of skin diseases, some of which were contagious, and some of which were even fatal. Lepers were generally cast out of regular society and considered "unclean" both religiously and socially. Priests served as the health inspectors who could certify that someone was cured or cleansed of leprosy and therefore "clean" for social contact.

5. *What action did Jesus take in this story to give the ten men with leprosy a glimpse of God's kingdom and glory and a "sample of heavenly fare"?*

6. *Which surprises you more: the behavior of the nine who went to the priests or the behavior of the one who went back to thank Jesus? Why does that surprise you more?*

7. *What did Jesus say about the one man who returned to thank Him? What does this reveal about the type of heart that God wants you to have toward Him?*

8. *What helps you to practice thankfulness? What are some of the "spiritual blessings" that have fallen "freely onto you" when you have chosen to have a thankful heart?*

Apply

The focus of this week's readings is on thankfulness. Each day, read the passage slowly, pausing to think about what is being said. Remember, this is your opportunity to meet with Jesus, tell Him about what you are facing, and choose to practice thankfulness in that situation.

Day 1

Read Psalm 69:29–33. *How does thanksgiving affect others who hear you offering it? How does this passage motivate you to engage in thankfulness?*

Day 2

Read 1 Thessalonians 5:18. *What do you think it means to give thanks "in all circumstances"? How is that possible for a person to do?*

Day 3

Read 1 Thessalonians 5:18 again. *What is a circumstance in which you are struggling (or have struggled) to give thanks to the Lord? Why do you think it is God's will for you to express gratitude to Him regardless of that circumstance?*

Day 4

Read Psalm 100:1–5. *What does it look like for you to "shout for joy to the* Lord*" (verse 1)? What are some of the most meaningful ways that God shows His faithfulness to you?*

Day 5

Read Psalm 107:1–5. *What is your "story" when it comes to God's goodness (verse 2)? What are some of the things for which you are "hungry and thirsty" (verse 5)?*

Day 6

Read Psalm 107:6–9. *Have you cried out to the Lord in your trouble? (If not, do so now!) What is the longing in your soul that you would like God to satisfy?*

Day 7

Read Psalm 107:10–16. *What can you thank God for today, even if He hasn't finished rescuing you? If you have been saved from your distress, who would benefit from hearing your grateful story of redemption? What is the key takeaway you would want to communicate?*

Week 27

FREEDOM IN FORGIVENESS

Discover

Living a life of worship means staying close to God and addressing the sins that can create distance between us and Him. Some of us feel guilt quickly and are aware of our faults, while others among us barely notice our mistakes. This sometimes is a reflection of our personality or our personal history, but it can also indicate our degree of sensitivity to God's Spirit.

In either case, remaining open to the Lord's leading in our spiritual development is essential. Whether we need to learn how to fully accept and trust His forgiveness or ask Him for greater awareness and conviction of sin, God is invested in helping us grow.

This week you will explore how regular self-examination and confession not only brings you closer to God but also leads to the freedom and peace found in His forgiveness.

1. *Do you tend to be blind to your faults or so acutely aware of them that you blame yourself most of the time?*

2. *In which area of your life has that tendency affected you the most?*

Experience

When your sins weigh heavily upon you, come to Me. Confess your wrongdoing, which I know all about before you say a word. Stay in the Light of My Presence, receiving forgiveness, cleansing, and healing. Remember that *I have clothed you in My righteousness*, so nothing can separate you from Me. Whenever you stumble or fall, I am there to help you up.

Man's tendency is to hide from his sin, seeking refuge in the darkness. There he indulges in self-pity, denial, self-righteousness, blaming, and hatred. But *I am the Light of the world*, and My illumination decimates the darkness. Come close to Me and let My Light envelop you, driving out darkness and permeating you with Peace.

– From *Jesus Calling*, May 20

3. *"When your sins weigh heavily upon you, come to Me." How easy is it for you to come to Christ for forgiveness? To what extent are you weighed down by unconfessed sin?*

4. *"Remember that I have clothed you in My righteousness." To what extent do you need to stop carrying around memories of old sins that have already been confessed and forgiven?*

DWELL

Read Psalm 32:1–11. God invites you to "stay in the Light of [His] Presence, receiving forgiveness, cleansing, and healing." In this psalm—one of the seven "penitential psalms" (the others are Psalms 6; 38; 51; 102; 130; 143)—David emphasizes the blessing of forgiveness and the relief that comes from confessing your sin. This psalm includes themes not only of repentance but also thanksgiving (see verses 3–8) and wisdom (see verses 1–2, 9–11).

5. *God's forgiveness "drives out darkness and permeates you with Peace." What are the blessings of forgiveness that David notes? How is life better when you are forgiven?*

6. *First John 1:8–9 reinforces David's psalm. The author states, "If we claim to be without sin, we deceive ourselves and the truth is not in us. If we confess our sins, [God] is faithful and just and will forgive us our sins." Have you ever felt that your sins were too "bad" for God to forgive? How did John address that feeling in this passage?*

7. *Our human tendency is to "hide from [our] sin, seeking refuge in the darkness." What does David say happened to him when he "kept silent" (verse 3) about his sin?*

8. *How are those who refuse to admit their sin like "the horse or the mule" (verse 9)? What might David be saying here about his own past stubbornness to admit his wrongdoing?*

Apply

The focus of this week's readings is on repentance and forgiveness. Each day, read the passage slowly, pausing to think about what God is saying to you. Remember, this is an opportunity to meet with Him, confess your sins, and experience the freedom that forgiveness provides.

Day 1

Read Psalm 32:8–11. *What do these verses from the psalmist tell you about how to live differently and overcome your habitual sins?*

Day 2

Read Psalm 51:1–4. *Why can you hope for mercy from God when you acknowledge your sins? How is mercy different from excusing or diminishing wrong behavior?*

Day 3

Read Psalm 51:7–12. *Why is it important to have a changed heart and spirit? What does forgiveness lead to?*

Day 4

Read Psalm 51:13–17. *What is it about forgiveness that moved the psalmist to praise the Lord? What kind of worship offering does God desire from you? Why?*

Day 5

Read Psalm 51:18–19. *What does it mean for you to "do good" (verse 18 NKJV)? In what areas of your life are you currently doing good as the psalmist instructs?*

Day 6

Read 1 John 3:16. *How would you describe the kind of love that John asks you to practice? What opportunities do you have for practicing this kind of love?*

Day 7

Read 1 John 3:17–18. *Sometimes you need God's forgiveness for the things you should be doing but haven't done. Talk with God about one or two ways that you have fallen short of showing His love to others. Is there some area in which you need forgiveness and a fresh start?*

Week 28

FALSE WORSHIP

Discover

Do you recognize false worship when you see it? False worship can involve turning to other religions or other forms of spirituality outside of faith in Christ. But more often, it comes in the form of placing your trust where it doesn't belong.

An idol can be defined as anything you fear, love, or depend on more than God. It might be a person you believe is essential to your happiness, money and the sense of security it so often creates, or achieving a level of influence or power that you've dreamed of having since childhood. Idols like these fight for the place in your heart that only God was meant to fill. Only devotion to the one true God will satisfy your soul.

In this week's study, you will reflect on what you might unknowingly be placing above God in your life and discover how to seek Him completely.

1. *Life depends on God, but what things are you most often tempted to put in His place?*

2. *What is so appealing about those particular things?*

Experience

Worship Me only. Idolatry has always been the downfall of My people. I make no secrets about being *a jealous God*. Current idols are more subtle than ancient ones because today's false gods are often outside the field of religion. People, possessions, status, and self-aggrandizement are some of the most popular deities today. Beware of bowing down before these things. False gods never satisfy; instead, they stir up lust for more and more.

When you seek Me instead of the world's idols, you experience My Joy and Peace. These intangibles slake the thirst of your soul, providing deep satisfaction. The glitter of the world is tinny and temporal. The Light of My Presence is brilliant and everlasting. Walk in the Light with Me. Thus you become a beacon through whom others are drawn to Me.

– From *Jesus Calling*, July 11

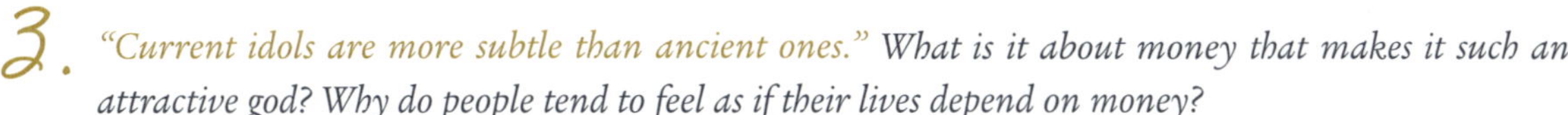

3. *"Current idols are more subtle than ancient ones." What is it about money that makes it such an attractive god? Why do people tend to feel as if their lives depend on money?*

4. *"False gods never satisfy; instead, they stir up lust for more and more." Given this reality, why is it critical to depend on God rather than people, possessions, or status?*

Dwell

Read Matthew 6:19–21, 24. The treasure of this world is "tinny and temporal," while the treasure of God's kingdom is "brilliant and everlasting." Jesus' advice is to seek after *eternal treasure*. He warns that "where your treasure is, there your heart will be also" (verse 21) and that "you cannot serve God and mammon" (verse 24 NKJV). (*Mammon* is a Greek word for material greed or wealth that was often personified as a false god.) Jesus' concern here is not about seeking money as a means of providing for your needs but about misplaced values. He is asking whether your heart is seeking after *God* or after *material wealth*.

5. *What are some "treasures on earth" (verse 19) that people often pursue? Why do these false gods "never satisfy" but only "stir up lust for more and more"?*

6. *How would you describe the "treasures in heaven" that Jesus asks you to pursue? Why does seeking after these kinds of treasures lead to deep satisfaction in your soul?*

7. *What are some of the "masters" (verse 24) the world compels you to serve? Where would you say your loyalties lie when it comes to whom you serve?*

8. *God has made "no secrets about being a jealous God." Given this, why is it actually impossible to claim your allegiance to God while serving anything or anyone else?*

Apply

The focus of this week's readings is on rejecting idols. Each day, read the passage slowly, pausing to consider and meditate on what is being said. Remember, this is an opportunity to meet with Jesus and lay any false idols that you have been serving at His feet.

Day 1

Read Isaiah 40:18–22. *What are the signs that something made by humans has become an idol to you? (Consider technology as an example.)*

Day 2

Read Isaiah 45:18–21. *The Lord says, "I have not spoken in secret" (verse 19). How have you experienced the truth of this statement? Why do some people feel like the Lord speaks in secret?*

Day 3

Read Isaiah 45:18–21 again. *Three times in these verses the Lord says there is no other God besides Him (see verses 18 and 21). Why do you think He repeats this assertion?*

Day 4

Read Romans 1:20–23. *What does it mean for a person's thinking to become "futile" (verse 21)? Do you believe it's possible to reject God and worship nothing, or does everybody worship something? Explain your response.*

Day 5

Read Psalm 24:1–6. *David refers to an idol in verse 4 as "what is false" (ESV). What blessings do the idols of this world falsely promise?*

Day 6

Read Psalm 36:5–9. *What reasons for trusting in God rather than idols does this passage offer? Which reason speaks most deeply to you today—and why?*

Day 7

Read Psalm 36:10–12. *How do you need God's justice? How do you need His faithfulness?*

Week 29

UNDER GOD'S GUIDANCE

Discover

One of our greatest comforts in this fallen world is that God is far greater than we can comprehend. Not one of our struggles or most pressing needs is beyond His wisdom or abilities. He invites us to trust Him fully, for His thoughts and plans surpass anything we can imagine. Instead of clinging to our own expectations, our own agendas, we are called to seek His guidance through prayer, Scripture, and aligning our hearts with His will.

This isn't wishful thinking. God commands His people to put their full trust in Him as a matter of obedience—an obedience that yields blessings. "If you obey me fully and keep my covenant, then out of all nations you will be my treasured possession. Although the whole earth is mine, you will be for me a kingdom of priests and a holy nation" (Exodus 19:5–6).

In this week's study, you will consider what it means to truly seek God's thoughts and ways, trusting that His perfect timing and purposes will accomplish far more than you could achieve on your own.

1. *What is your typical attitude toward planning? Do you like to plan ahead in detail or do you prefer to be more spontaneous? Explain your response.*

2. *What steps do you take to make sure your plans for the future are aligned with God's plans for your future?*

Experience

Thank Me in the midst of the crucible. When things seem all wrong, look for growth opportunities. Especially look for areas where you need to let go, leaving your cares in My able hands. Do you trust Me to orchestrate your life events as I choose, or are you still trying to make things go according to your will? If you keep trying to carry out your intentions while I am leading you in another direction, you deify your desires.

Be on the lookout for what I am doing in your life. Worship Me by living close to Me, *thanking Me in all circumstances.*

— From *Jesus Calling*, May 13

3. *"Look for areas where you need to let go." What attitude should you have when it comes to planning? How would you rate your ability to let go of control and trust God?*

4. *"Be on the lookout for what I am doing in your life." How do you go about being on the lookout for the way in which God is guiding you through a day?*

Dwell

Read Isaiah 55:6–11. In this passage, the Lord basically asks His people, "Do you trust Me to orchestrate your life events as I choose?" The people had been found guilty of relying on their own wisdom and following their own path—which had led to wickedness and unrighteousness. Now, the invitation was to seek Him "while he is near" (verse 6), emphasizing they could still turn to Him for mercy and forgiveness. God's ways and thoughts are higher than our own. His Word, like rain and snow, will accomplish its purpose, bringing forth life and prosperity.

5. *Much like the Israelites, it's easy to fall prey to "deify[ing] your desires." Think of a decision you're currently trying to make. What would getting your way look like in that situation?*

6. *What might it look like for God to get His way in that situation? Although you can't know for sure, what do you think God's desires and purposes might be for you?*

7. *What does God say about the nature of His thoughts and ways as compared to the thoughts and ways of humankind? What does this say about whom you should trust?*

8. *Sometimes you might not "trust [God] to orchestrate your life events" because you fear that He won't come through for you. What does God say about the "word" that goes from His mouth (verse 11)? What promise does He give to you about keeping His word?*

Apply

The focus of this week's readings is on seeking God's will and His ways. Each day, read the passage slowly, pausing to think about what is being said and to reflect on the truths being shared. Remember, this is an opportunity to meet with God and submit your plans to Him.

Day 1

Read Psalm 119:9–14. *What is your prime source for knowing how to seek after God with all your heart? According to this passage, what are the benefits of this source?*

Day 2

Read Psalm 119:15–16. *What does it mean to meditate on God's precepts? What are the benefits of doing this?*

Day 3

Read Luke 6:20–23. *In what ways do you identify with those whom Jesus said are blessed?*

Day 4

Read Luke 6:24–26. *How would you describe the meaning of woe in this passage? Who did Jesus warn—and why did He warn them?*

Day 5

Read Luke 6:27–31. *What is the kind of life that Jesus describes in this passage? How can you put these commands into practice?*

Day 6

Read Luke 6:32–36. *What reasons for loving your enemies does Jesus provide in these verses? What are the risks of doing this? Why are these risks worth it?*

Day 7

Read Matthew 20:1–16. *What did Jesus mean when He said, "So the last will be first, and the first will be last" (verse 16)? What do His words mean to you?*

Week 30

STAY CLOSE!

Discover

A life of worship is about *staying close to God*. It's not always easy to focus on Him in the rush of daily life. After all, you have places to go, decisions to navigate, and commitments to fulfill. But as you make a habit of turning to the Lord, communing with Him becomes second nature.

The goal is to carry Him in your heart throughout the day—sending up brief prayers for guidance, whispers of gratitude, or simply calling on Jesus' name. In time, this connection deepens, and He becomes your first thought in times of need or celebration.

In this study, you will explore how practicing this closeness can transform your relationship with God, and you will also look at some of the opportunities it presents to you.

1. *What are the biggest distractions in your life that take your mind away from God and the other things you most need to think about?*

2. *What two words could you whisper throughout the day to realign your mind and heart with God? How can you remind yourself to recite these words?*

Experience

Worship Me by living close to Me. This was My original design for man, into whom *I breathed My very breath of Life*. This is My desire for you: that you stay near Me as you walk along your life-path. Each day is an important part of that journey. Although you may feel as if you are going nowhere in this world, your spiritual journey is another matter altogether, taking you along steep, treacherous paths of adventure. That is why *walking in the Light of My Presence* is essential to keep you from stumbling. By staying close to Me, you present yourself as a *living sacrifice*. Even the most routine part of your day can be *a spiritual act of worship, holy and pleasing to Me*.

— From *Jesus Calling*, September 14

3. *"Worship Me by living close to Me." What does living close to God look like in your life?*

4. *"Stay near Me as you walk along your life-path." What things tend to get in the way of you walking closely with God? How can you overcome those things?*

DWELL

Read John 15:1–9. "Walking in the Light of [Christ's] Presence" and "living close" to Him involves more than just a once-in-a-while interaction. As Jesus explains in this passage, the relationship is intended to be one in which His followers are *continually* abiding in Him. Jesus uses the metaphor of a vine and branches to emphasize this act of abiding in Him, like a branch on a vine, is essential for bearing fruit and experiencing His love and peace.

5. *Jesus calls Himself "the true vine" and His Father "the gardener" (verse 1). What is the role of the branches? What does the Gardener expect of them?*

6. *What does Jesus say is the secret of how the branches can bear good fruit? What does it mean in practical terms to "remain" or "abide" (NKJV) in Jesus?*

7. *Jesus says, "Apart from me you can do nothing" (verse 5). The idea is to travel side by side with Him if you want to keep progressing on "your spiritual journey." When have you found it to be true that you can do nothing outside of Christ? Describe the situation.*

8. *What happens to the branches that do not remain in the vine? What is Jesus saying about the kind of people who choose to pursue their own way in life?*

Apply

The focus of this week's readings is on remaining close to God. Each day, read the passage slowly, pausing to reflect on what is being said. Remember, this is your opportunity to connect with Jesus and carry Him with you in your heart throughout the day.

Day 1

Read Psalm 143:5–8. *How great is your thirst for God? How does that thirst affect the way you live? If you don't thirst for Him that much, then why do you think that is the case?*

Day 2

Read Exodus 13:20–22. *What guidance do you need in your life right now? How can you remain in God so that you are alert to receive His direction?*

Day 3

Read Psalm 119:33–36. *What are some of the ways the psalmist says that he cultivates closeness with God? Which of those ways resonate with you—and why?*

Day 4

Read Psalm 119:37–40. *Why is it important to do the things God has commanded?*

Day 5

Read John 15:10–11. *How do you remain in Jesus' love and abide in Him?*

Day 6

Read John 15:12–13. *Which command does Jesus single out in these verses? Why do you think this command is so essential to living close to Him?*

Day 7

Read John 15:14–17. *How does this passage explain the fruit that Jesus wants you to bear? Why is this fruit important?*

Week 31

HOLY AND BEAUTIFUL

DISCOVER

The psalmist wrote, "Worship the LORD in the beauty of holiness!" (Psalm 96:9 NKJV). That phrase, "the beauty of holiness," is rich with meaningful reminders.

First, holiness is inherently beautiful. Such sacred purity, righteousness, and excellence are beyond compare. Second, holiness reveals something profound about God's nature. Anything truthful, good, noble, glorious, or lovely is of Him and from Him. Third, as you grow in godliness, your life becomes more and more beautiful and pleasing to the Lord.

When you "worship the LORD in the beauty of holiness," you not only honor His perfection but also recognize His beauty reflected in the world and within yourself. In this study, you will be invited to look at God's holiness in this light and to see His beauty as a reminder of both His presence and your worth.

1. *What are three words you associate with beauty as it relates to the outside world (for example, sunsets, beaches, mountains)?*

2. *What are three words you associate with beauty as it relates to yourself (for example, physical looks, intelligence, likability)?*

Experience

Worship Me *in the beauty of holiness.* All true beauty reflects some of who I am. I am working My ways in you: the divine Artist creating loveliness within your being. My main work is to clear out debris and clutter, making room for My Spirit to take full possession. Collaborate with Me in this effort by being willing to let go of anything I choose to take away. I know what you need, and I have promised to provide all of that—abundantly!

Your sense of security must not rest in your possessions or in things going your way. I am training you to depend on Me alone, finding fulfillment in My Presence. This entails being satisfied with much or with little, accepting *either* as My will for the moment. Instead of grasping and controlling, you are learning to release and receive. Cultivate this receptive stance by trusting Me in every situation.

— From *Jesus Calling*, November 7

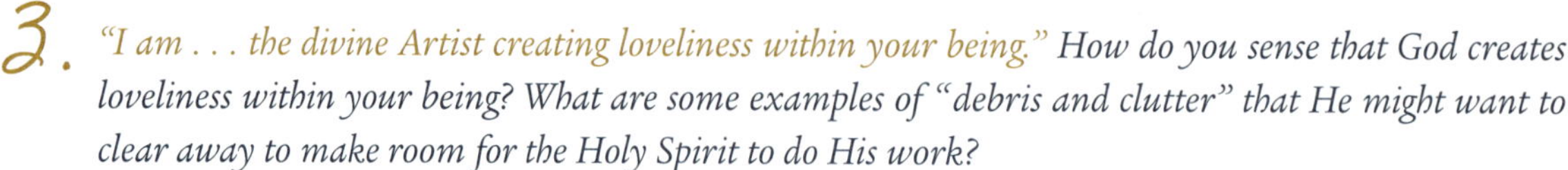

3. *"I am . . . the divine Artist creating loveliness within your being." How do you sense that God creates loveliness within your being? What are some examples of "debris and clutter" that He might want to clear away to make room for the Holy Spirit to do His work?*

4. *"I am training you to depend on Me alone." What is a circumstance you are currently facing in which you need to depend on God alone rather than on things going your way?*

Dwell

Read Psalm 96:1–13. This psalm, written by an unknown author, is a call to recognize God as "the divine Artist" who desires for His people to "worship [Him] in the beauty of holiness." The psalmist urges all people—and all creation—to acknowledge God's greatness and sovereignty, give Him glory, and proclaim "his salvation from day to day" (verse 2 ESV).

5. *What does the psalmist call on "all the earth" (verse 1) to do? What are people everywhere to recognize about "the beauty of holiness" that is represented in God?*

6. *What does the psalmist mean when he writes that God "is to be feared above all gods" (verse 4)? What reasons do you have to feel awe when you enter the Lord's presence?*

7. *What does it mean for the heavens, the earth, the sea, the fields, and the trees to join in rejoicing before the Lord (see verses 11–12)? How does the natural world worship Him?*

8. *What overall image does the psalmist present of the Lord? Given His divine nature and power, why is it foolish to put "your sense of security" in anything other than Him?*

Apply

The focus of this week's readings is on the Lord's beauty and the impact it makes on us. Each day, read the passage slowly, pausing to reflect on what is being said. Remember, this is an opportunity to meet with God and explore what Scripture says about His beauty and holiness.

Day 1

Read Psalm 19:1–6. *In which ways are you moved to praise God when you see His creation?*

Day 2

Read Exodus 34:29–35. *How does this passage help you understand the beauty of holiness?*

Day 3

Read 2 Corinthians 3:7–9. *Have you ever seen someone who is radiant with righteousness? If so, what did that look like? If not, what do you imagine that would look like?*

Day 4

Read 2 Corinthians 3:18. *What are some practices involved in contemplating the Lord's glory? Why is such contemplation invaluable?*

Day 5

Read Psalm 29:1–9. *What does it mean to ascribe glory to the Lord? How is that done?*

Day 6

Read Hebrews 13:15. *What does the writer mean when he refers to "the fruit of our lips" (NKJV)? In what circumstances do you find you can easily speak praise to God?*

Day 7

Read 1 Chronicles 16:23–25. *Write a statement of praise for today to the Lord your God.*

Week 32

OVERFLOWING WITH GRATITUDE

Discover

David writes in Psalm 23:5 that his "cup overflows" when he considers the goodness of God. The imagery is of the Lord pouring such an abundance into David's "cup" (his life) that it can't be contained but spills out over the sides.

When we, like David, reflect on all the blessings the Lord has poured into our lives, it should naturally compel us toward gratitude. The greater our gratitude, the more our hearts fill up to overflowing. Before we know it, we are being drawn into worship of the One who alone is worthy of our reverence. As we increasingly focus on God's goodness and provision, we can't help but worship from a genuine, joyful place within us. This joy is one of the many gifts of abundant life in Him for all who are redeemed.

In this week's study, you will explore what it looks like to have a heart overflowing with gratitude toward God and how that posture can open you up to greater intimacy with Him.

1. *When in your life can you recall overflowing with gratitude toward the Lord?*

2. *How would you describe what it means to live a life of worship?*

Experience

WHEN YOU WORSHIP ME *in spirit and truth*, you join with choirs of angels who are continually before My throne. Though you cannot hear their voices, your praise and thanksgiving are distinctly audible in heaven. Your petitions are also heard, but it is your gratitude that clears the way to My Heart. With the way between us wide open, My blessings fall upon you in rich abundance. The greatest blessing is nearness to Me—abundant Joy and Peace in My Presence. Practice praising and thanking Me continually throughout this day.

– From *Jesus Calling*, July 4

3. *"It is your gratitude that clears the way to My Heart." Why do you think gratitude is so important to God? How does it clear the way to His heart?*

4. *"Practice praising and thanking Me continually." What are some ways you have found to be effective in incorporating gratitude to God throughout the day?*

Dwell

Read John 12:1–8 and reflect on the statement, "When you worship Me in spirit and truth, you join with choirs of angels who are continually before My throne." As you read, note that this story takes place less than a week before Jesus' arrest and execution. Jesus knows these events are coming, but His disciples don't want to believe it. The group has gathered together in Bethany to have dinner with a family who has a good reason for gratitude. Martha and Mary are the sisters of Lazarus, whom Jesus had recently raised from the dead.

5. *Mary poured "an expensive perfume" on Jesus' feet and "wiped his feet with her hair" (verse 3), which was an act of humility and devotion. What does this say about the kind of worship that God desires? How is worship both costly and humbling on the part of the worshiper?*

6. *Judas complained that Mary's act of worship was wasteful. What does Jesus' response reveal about what God sees as valuable when it comes to worship of Him?*

7. *What does Jesus say that Mary was also doing in this moment (see verse 7)? What does this say about your acts of worship being "distinctly audible in heaven"?*

8. *What does the kind of passionate worship that Mary expressed look like for you?*

Apply

The focus of this week's readings is on the impact of gratitude. Each day, read the passage slowly, pausing to think about what is being said. Remember, this is an opportunity to meet with the Lord and express the gratitude toward Him that is overflowing from your heart.

Day 1

Read Psalm 121:1–8. *As majestic as the mountains are, the psalmist knows his help comes from Someone even more majestic. What reasons do you have for looking to God alone for your help? How does this move your heart toward gratitude for all that He has done for you?*

Day 2

Read Psalm 121:1–8 again. *What circumstances do you need to know the Lord is watching over in your life? What does this psalm reveal about God's nature and character?*

Day 3

Read Psalm 122:1–9. *This psalm is about gathering with others in the house of the Lord to express your praise, worship, and gratitude to Him. Why is this important?*

Day 4

Read Psalm 123:1–4. *The psalmist writes about looking to the Lord for mercy. What acts of mercy has God given to you? How does remembering His goodness move you to gratitude?*

Day 5

Read Psalm 124:1–8. *Think of a "flood" that threatened you in the past that God saved you from. Write out a prayer of thanksgiving to Him for His deliverance.*

Day 6

Read Psalm 124:1–8 again. *How has the Lord been on your side? How does He show that He is on your side even when you don't always get your way?*

Day 7

Read Psalm 125:1–5. *In what area do you need to trust in the Lord right now? How can you express your gratitude to Him for His promises to care and provide for you?*

Week 33

STRONG AND COURAGEOUS

DISCOVER

No one likes going through "storms" in life. Storms are unpredictable. They can disrupt our world and take us to places we didn't expect to go. Often these are uncomfortable places where we must depend on God to guide us to the other side.

As much as we might wish otherwise, God's path doesn't always lead directly to green pastures but also takes us through valleys that test our faith (see Psalm 23:4). Feeling fear in such times of uncertainty is a natural response. But courage, strengthened by God's promises, is what supernaturally helps us to move forward with peace in our hearts.

Repeatedly, the Israelites experienced the strengthening effects of relying on God as well as the disastrous effects of failing to trust Him. This week, you will step into their shoes and explore the risks they were asked to take as they journeyed toward the promised land. You'll reflect on their fears, God's words to them, and the relevance of those words for you.

1. *Which images come to your mind when you think about what it means to have courage?*

2. *What sorts of individuals or endeavors come to mind when you think about being courageous in the face of fear?*

Experience

Do not be afraid, for I am with you. Hear Me saying *"Peace, be still,"* to your restless heart. No matter what happens, *I will never leave you or forsake you.* Let this assurance soak into your mind and heart until you overflow with Joy. *Though the earth give way and the mountains fall into the heart of the sea*, you need not fear!

The media relentlessly proclaim bad news: for breakfast, lunch, and dinner. A steady diet of their fare will sicken you. Instead of focusing on fickle, ever-changing news broadcasts, tune in to the living Word—the One who is always the same. Let Scripture saturate your mind and heart, and you will walk steadily along the path of Life. Even though you don't know what will happen tomorrow, you can be absolutely sure of your ultimate destination. *I hold you by your right hand, and afterward I will take you into Glory.*

– From *Jesus Calling*, April 20

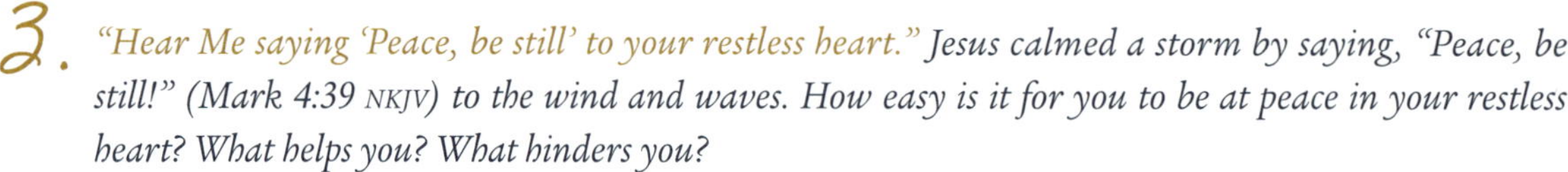

3. *"Hear Me saying 'Peace, be still' to your restless heart." Jesus calmed a storm by saying, "Peace, be still!" (Mark 4:39 NKJV) to the wind and waves. How easy is it for you to be at peace in your restless heart? What helps you? What hinders you?*

4. *"Let Scripture saturate your mind and heart." How does tuning in to the Word of God build up your courage in the midst of society's constant and incessant barrage of bad news?*

Dwell

Read Deuteronomy 31:1–8. God had called Moses to confront Pharaoh and lead the Israelites out of slavery in Egypt. Moses had gone out on a limb and obeyed God, but when the people refused to conquer the promised land, he was forced to wander with them for forty years in the desert. The events in this passage take place toward the end of that time when the people were finally ready to enter the promised land. God had appointed Joshua to lead the invasion and Moses, nearing the end of his life, wanted them to know that God would not leave them nor forsake them. They could "let this assurance soak into [their] mind and heart."

5. *Who did Moses say would "cross over ahead" (verse 3) of the people? How should this have filled the Israelites with courage as they listened to Moses' message?*

6. *God was communicating to His people, "Do not be afraid, for I am with you." What did the Israelites need the strength and courage to do? What did Joshua need the strength and courage to do?*

7. *What do you need courage to do? How can God's promises help you in this situation?*

8. *What did Moses remind the people about God's promises to their ancestors in the past? How do you think this would have helped the people prepare for the task before them?*

Apply

The focus of this week's readings is on adding strength to courage. Each day, read the passage slowly, pausing to think about what is being said and the truths that are being revealed. Remember, this is an opportunity to meet with the Lord and reflect on His faithfulness to you.

Day 1

Read Deuteronomy 31:23. *Moses had previously instructed the people and Joshua to "be strong and courageous" (verses 6–7) because the Lord promised to be with them. What was the significance of God again giving this instruction to Joshua?*

Day 2

Read Joshua 1:6–7. *What did God specifically instruct Joshua to do as the people prepared to enter the promised land? Why do you think God once again repeated this command to Joshua?*

Day 3

Read Psalm 89:1–4. *When have you experienced God's faithfulness toward you personally? What, if anything, did that do to strengthen your courage for future situations?*

Day 4

Read Psalm 89:5–8. *The psalmist speaks of God's faithfulness two more times in these verses. Why do you think the biblical writer repeatedly spoke of this characteristic of God?*

Day 5

Read Psalm 89:9–13. *Where do you see God's power at work in the world around you? What about His power at work in your life?*

Day 6

Read Psalm 89:14–18. *The psalmist finds courage when he remembers that God is his "shield" and "king" (verse 18). What is strengthening your courage right now?*

Day 7

Read Psalm 27:14. *When have you waited on the Lord to the point that it was almost unbearable? How did you find your courage to continue to wait?*

Week 34

CONFRONTING CHALLENGES

DISCOVER

Sometimes we face challenges that feel far bigger than we can handle. We may find ourselves doubting if we have the strength or the faith to follow through with what God is asking of us. The task seems immense and we feel small in comparison.

But the Bible shows us that this exact scenario happens time and again to those whom God has called. It's not a mistake; it's part of His plan. God intentionally places us in situations where we must rely on Him so that His power and glory are unmistakable. He doesn't expect us to fight our fears alone. Instead, He invites us to trust Him completely.

In this week's study, you will explore a well-known Bible story that highlights this truth and discover how trusting in God equips you to face life's challenges with confidence.

1. *When have you encountered a challenge that felt too big for you? Did you meet the challenge, try but not quite make it, or just back away and not try? Explain your response.*

2. *Think of a challenge where you called on the Lord to strengthen you because you knew that you could not overcome it without Him. How did that differ from trying to overcome something on your own?*

Experience

TRUST ME AND DON'T BE AFRAID, *for I am your Strength and Song.* Think what it means to have Me as your Strength. I spoke the universe into existence; My Power is absolutely unlimited! Human weakness, consecrated to Me, is like a magnet, drawing My Power into your neediness. However, fear can block the flow of My Strength into you. Instead of trying to fight your fears, concentrate on trusting Me. When you relate to Me in confident trust, there is no limit to how much I can strengthen you.

Remember that I am also your Song. I want you to share My Joy, living in conscious awareness of My Presence. Rejoice as we journey together toward heaven; join Me in singing My Song.

– From *Jesus Calling*, March 21

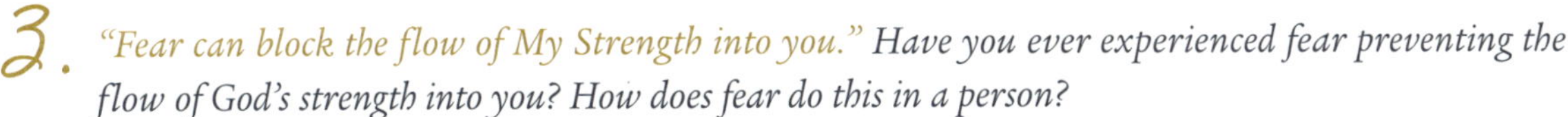

3. *"Fear can block the flow of My Strength into you." Have you ever experienced fear preventing the flow of God's strength into you? How does fear do this in a person?*

4. *"Instead of trying to fight your fears, concentrate on trusting Me." Why is it better to focus your efforts on trusting in God rather than trying to fight your fears?*

Dwell

Read 1 Samuel 17:1–50. This famous story of David versus Goliath is a testament to "how much [God] can strengthen you" when you "relate to [Him] in confident trust." At the time, David was a shepherd of Israel who was tending his father's flocks. Goliath was a giant of man and an experienced soldier of Philistia who had struck fear into the hearts of the Israelites for forty days. Note that this story involves a form of warfare prevalent at the time in which champions from opposing armies would fight on behalf of their nations. The outcome of the battle between the champions would determine which nation was deemed victorious.

5. *Fear can "block the flow of [God's] Strength into you." How did the Israelites' fear of Goliath block the flow of God's Strength into them as an army? Why do you think none of the Israelites—the king included—appears to have looked to God in this situation?*

6. *What attitude did David have when he arrived at the battlefront? What belief did he have that the Lord God could deliver the Israelites from the Philistines?*

7. *What gave David courage to approach King Saul and ask to fight the Philistine? What does David say about his sources of courage in verses 34–37 and 45–47?*

8. *Why does God often choose to work through an "ordinary" person—someone who isn't obviously the strongest one in an area of endeavor (see verse 47)?*

Apply

The focus of this week's reading is on acting in faith when you are feeling weak or timid. Each day, read the passage slowly, pausing to think about what is being said. Remember, this is an opportunity to meet with Jesus and reflect on the strength that He provides to you.

Day 1

Read 2 Corinthians 12:6–9. *The nature of Paul's "thorn in the flesh" (verse 7* NKJV*) is not known. However, what does he say here about its function in his life? What are your biggest weaknesses? Can you imagine boasting about them? Explain your response.*

Day 2

Read 2 Corinthians 12:10. *What does Paul say in this verse about his weaknesses and difficulties? What might be some of the ways your weaknesses are bringing glory to God?*

Day 3

Read Luke 1:26–38. *Knowing that nothing is impossible for God, what will you be brave enough to do today in obedience to Him, in spite of any trepidation you may have?*

Day 4

Read Isaiah 12:2–3. *What reason does Isaiah offer for not being afraid? What reasons does he offer for having joy? How does joy contribute to greater faith?*

Day 5

Read Isaiah 12:4–6. *Why is it important to "make known among the nations" (verse 4) what God has done?*

Day 6

Read 2 Timothy 1:5–8. *Where does Paul say Timothy could get the courage to join him in suffering for the gospel? Would you be willing to suffer for the gospel? Why or why not?*

Day 7

Read Psalm 27:1, Proverbs 28:1, and 2 Timothy 1:7. *How do these verses encourage you when it comes to confronting challenges?*

Week 35

SECURITY IN GOD

Discover

Trusting God is not always easy. When the world tempts us to compromise our faith, for example, standing firm in God's plan can sometimes cost us a relationship, a job, or an opportunity. But in those moments, we must remind ourselves that our security doesn't come from others or our circumstances. It rests in God alone.

Choosing God above all else takes faith. *Real* faith. It means saying, "God comes first. His purpose is what matters most. I will not waver just because someone has the power to make things difficult for me." It means believing that "in all things God works for the good of those who love him, who have been called according to his purpose" (Romans 8:28).

In this week's study, you will explore the inspiring story of three young men who boldly placed their trust in God above everything else. You will also discover what their example teaches us about remaining faithful to the Lord even in the most challenging times.

1. *Have you ever known someone who acted as if he or she wanted to have the place of God? If so, what did that person do that made it seem that way?*

2. *How did you respond to that person? What did it cost you to put God first?*

Experience

I WANT YOU TO BE ALL MINE. I am weaning you from other dependencies. Your security rests in Me alone—not in other people, not in circumstances. Depending only on Me may feel like walking on a tightrope, but there is a safety net underneath: *the everlasting arms*. So don't be afraid of falling. Instead, look ahead to Me. I am always before you, beckoning you on—one step at a time. *Neither height nor depth, nor anything else in all creation, can separate you from My loving Presence.*

– From *Jesus Calling*, January 21

3. *"I am weaning you from other dependencies." What are ways you have witnessed God eliminating unhealthy dependencies in your life?*

4. *"I am always before you, beckoning you on—one step at a time." Why does depending on God often require a one-step-at-a-time kind of faith as He beckons you on?*

Dwell

Read Daniel 3:1–30. King Nebuchadnezzar of Babylon had been permitted by God to conquer Judah and take the Jewish people into captivity. Among those captives were Shadrach, Meshach, and Abednego. These three young men faced pressure to conform to a foreign government's demands that included worshiping pagan gods. Yet they remained steadfast in trusting God—even though it must have seemed they were "walking on a tightrope" of faith. Ultimately, God revealed that His "everlasting arms" were wide enough to catch them.

5. *As the story opens, what dilemma were Shadrach, Meshach, and Abednego facing? What pressure was on them to conform and worship the image of gold?*

6. *How did Shadrach, Meshach, and Abednego demonstrate their security rested in God alone? What did they recognize about the God whom they served (see verses 17–18)?*

7. *What is the significance of Nebuchadnezzar seeing a fourth man who looked "like a son of the gods" (verse 25) walking around in the fire with the three other men?*

8. *The story has a happy ending, but the three young men were prepared for it not to end that way. Even today, when God's people are persecuted for their faith, they face the very real possibility of tragedy. Given this, why is it still important for you to put your full trust in God even when you don't know what the outcome of your choices will be?*

Apply

The focus of this week's readings is on choosing to trust God. Each day, read the passage slowly, pausing to consider what is being said. Remember, this is an opportunity to meet with Jesus and express that you choose to completely trust in His will and way in your life.

Day 1

Read Matthew 10:16–20. *What does it mean to be a "sheep among wolves" (verse 16)? Why would Jesus ever ask you to put yourself in such a position?*

Day 2

Read Matthew 10:21–23. *What does Jesus say that His followers can expect in this world? How do Jesus' words affect you emotionally?*

Day 3

Read Matthew 10:21–23 again. *The type of conflict and persecution that Jesus describes is happening to Christians in many countries around the world today. How can you support them in prayer? How can you support them in other ways?*

Day 4

Read Matthew 10:24–25. *What does Jesus say you should expect when it comes to how others treat you because of your faith? Is it a bad sign if nobody is against you? Why or why not?*

Day 5

Read Matthew 10:26–31. *When Jesus said, "There is nothing concealed that will not be disclosed" (verse 26), He was stating that the truth of the gospel will always be revealed in the end. Why is this so empowering for Christ's followers in proclaiming His message?*

Day 6

Read Matthew 10:32–33. *How do Jesus' words parallel what Shadrach, Meshach, and Abednego understood about their Lord God (see Daniel 3:16–18)?*

Day 7

Read Matthew 10:34–39. *What do you think Jesus means when He says, "Anyone who loves their father or mother more than me is not worthy of me" (verse 37)? What does this say about putting God first and acknowledging Him before others? How do you do this?*

Week 36

COURAGEOUS COMMITMENT

Discover

Envy is a destructive force. It doesn't just long for what someone else has but begrudges that person for having it—sometimes to the point of wishing him or her harm.

The truth is, the more you grow in character and godliness, the more you may encounter those who look at your good qualities and resist them with malice. However, as you will discover in this week's reading, such reactions are not cause for despair. In fact, they are opportunities to lean into trust and courage.

This week, you will look at how the prophet Daniel was confronted with malice and envy. Yet in spite of the jealous schemes of those around him, he did not falter in his commitment to the Lord. His courage in the midst of opposition stands as a powerful example of how to walk with integrity and trust no matter how great the challenges are. You *can* have godly courage and remain firm in your faith even when others stand against you.

1. *You are now more than halfway through this study. Have you noticed yourself stepping out in faith more than you did before you began? If so, in what ways?*

2. *Think about the ways you have stepped out in faith—whether you consider them great or small. How have those acts on your part made you more courageous?*

Experience

IF YOU LEARN TO TRUST ME—really trust Me—with your whole being, then nothing can separate you from My Peace. Everything you endure can be put to good use by allowing it to train you in trusting Me. This is how you foil the works of evil, growing in grace through the very adversity that was meant to harm you. Joseph was a prime example of this divine reversal, declaring to his brothers: *"You meant evil against me, but God meant it for good."*

Do not fear what this day, or any day, may bring your way. Concentrate on trusting Me and on doing what needs to be done. Relax in My sovereignty, remembering that I go before you, as well as with you, into each day. *Fear no evil*, for I can bring good out of every situation you will ever encounter.

— From *Jesus Calling*, May 7

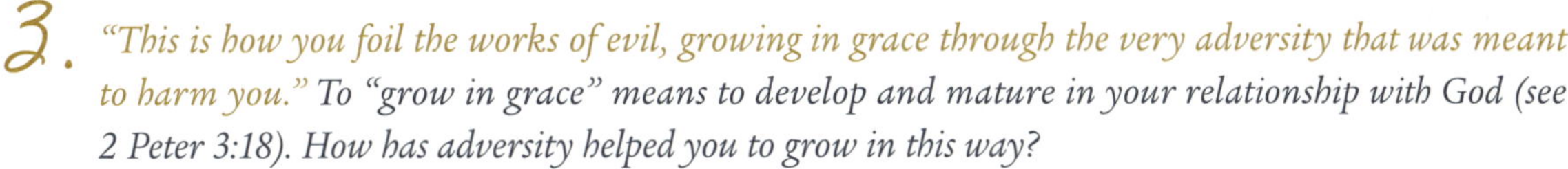

3. *"This is how you foil the works of evil, growing in grace through the very adversity that was meant to harm you." To "grow in grace" means to develop and mature in your relationship with God (see 2 Peter 3:18). How has adversity helped you to grow in this way?*

4. *"Relax in My sovereignty, remembering that I go before you." How is courage related to trust? How is it related to "relaxing" in God's sovereignty?*

Dwell

Read Daniel 6:1–24. The story of Daniel in the lions' den is a poignant illustration of what it means to "really trust [God] with your whole being." When Daniel's faithfulness to God came under attack, the jealous officials of Darius plotted against him, using the king's vanity and flawed laws to trap him. The punishment these officials devised of having Daniel thrown into a lions' den (literally an underground pit) was unheard of in the ancient Near East, revealing the extreme depths of their hatred toward him. Regardless, Daniel was determined to trust in God, and his miraculous rescue highlighted the Lord's ability to save and deliver His people.

5. *What brought about the administrators' and the satraps' attempt to find grounds for charges against Daniel? What does it say about his character that they could find none?*

6. *When Daniel learned about the decrees, what lawful alternatives did he have that would have spared his life? Why didn't he just stop his private worship for the thirty days?*

7. *Daniel was one who believed God would "go before [him], as well as with [him], into each day." How do you think this gave him the courage to face the lions' den?*

8. *How did the Lord "foil the works of evil" in this story? What did King Darius come to see about God's sovereign authority because Daniel was willing to trust in Him?*

Apply

The focus of this week's readings is on having courage and staying committed to the Lord in the face of bullying, envy, or hostility from others. Each day, read the passage slowly, pausing to think about what is being said. Remember, this is an opportunity to meet with Jesus.

Day 1

Read Psalm 27:2–3. *What terrifying situation does David describe in these verses? How do you think he was able to stand firm in his faith in spite of these circumstances?*

Day 2

Read Psalm 27:4–6. *What does David acknowledge in these verses about God's protection over his life? How do you think this helped him to remain courageous?*

Day 3

Read Psalm 27:7. *What is it that you want God to know about the situation you are in right now? How can you, like David, be confident that He will hear you?*

Day 4

Read Psalm 27:8–10. *What does it mean to seek God's face? How can you do that today?*

Day 5

Read Psalm 27:11–12. *How does knowing God's ways lead to a straight path?*

Day 6

Read Psalm 27:13–14. *What does waiting on the Lord have to do with being courageous? Why is it often a courageous act to simply wait on God?*

Day 7

Read Deuteronomy 33:26–29. *How has God proven to be your "refuge" (verse 27) and made you "live in safety" (verse 28)? How has He proven to be your "shield" and "sword" (verse 29)?*

Week 37

SPEAKING TRUTH

Discover

King Solomon wrote, "There is a time for everything, and a season for every activity under the heavens . . . a time to be silent and a time to speak" (Ecclesiastes 3:1, 7). There are moments when we are called to "be silent" and accept what is. Yet there are also moments that demand us to be bold, stand firm, and "speak," especially in the face of injustice.

True faith is demonstrated when we take the steps that God calls us to take during such times in life. Sometimes a step of faith can be as daunting as speaking truth to power. Yet it's in those moments of bravery that we witness God work in extraordinary ways.

In this week's study, you will examine the story of a courageous woman who didn't stay silent when it mattered most. Her brave actions in a dangerous situation serve as a powerful reminder of how God can work through those who are willing to speak up and act in faith.

1. *When you were a child, did you speak up and ask for what you needed (maybe even in a demanding way)? Or did you tend to more passively accept whatever happened?*

2. *What are some ways you would like to be bolder when it comes to standing up for others?*

Experience

WALK BY FAITH, NOT BY SIGHT. As you take steps of faith, depending on Me, I will show you how much I can do for you. If you live your life too safely, you will never know the thrill of seeing Me work through you. When I gave you My Spirit, I empowered you to live beyond your natural ability and strength. That's why it is so wrong to measure your energy level against the challenges ahead of you. The issue is not your strength but Mine, which is limitless. By walking close to Me, you can accomplish My purposes in My strength.

– From *Jesus Calling*, March 11

3. *"Walk by faith, not by sight." What does it mean to do this in your life? What is scary or unsettling to you about living your life this way?*

4. *"I empowered you to live beyond your natural ability and strength." What is the problem with living your life based only on what you feel you can do in your own strength?*

DWELL

Read Esther 4:1–17. This passage relates a conversation that took place (through attendants) between Esther, the queen of Persia, and Mordecai, her cousin. The story reveals that if "you live your life too safely"—afraid to take risks or exercise your faith—"you will never know the thrill of seeing [God] work through you." Truly the challenges in front of you will often be the richest opportunities to grow deeper in trust and fulfill God's greater purpose.

5. *The news that Mordecai heard "of all that had been done" (verse 1) was an edict sentencing all the Jewish people to death. What actions did Mordecai take when he discovered this edict was in place? What did he likely know would happen when he went to the king's gate?*

6. *What did Esther understand about going before the Persian king without being summoned? How did she demonstrate that she was willing to "walk by faith, not by sight"?*

7. *Esther was in just the right place at just the right time to speak up on behalf of the Jews. Where are you in just the right place when it comes to helping others?*

8. *This story never mentions God or even prayer. Yet where do you see Him in this account? What "thrill of seeing [God] work" did Esther witness as a result of her courage?*

Apply

The focus of this week's readings is on having the courage to stand up for the needs of others. Each day, read the passage slowly, pausing to think about what is being said and the truths that are being spoken to your heart. Remember, this is an opportunity to meet with Jesus and consider where He might be asking you to take a greater stand on behalf of others.

Day 1

Read Mark 5:21–24. *Why did Jairus need courage in this situation? What risk was he taking in seeking out Jesus for help?*

Day 2

Read Mark 5:35–36. *Jairus received some bad news on his way back home. What courage did he need in this situation? How did Jesus help provide that for him?*

Day 3

Read Mark 5:37–43. *What was the outcome of this story when Jesus arrived at Jairus's home? What do you think would have happened if Jairus had allowed fear to take over?*

Day 4

Read Psalm 31:19–24. *The psalmist speaks in verse 19 about fearing the Lord. How is fearing God consistent with courage? How do you demonstrate courage when you fear the Lord?*

Day 5

Read Philippians 1:27–30. *How does Paul describe courageous living in this passage?*

Day 6

Read Isaiah 41:8–13. *Do you believe God when He says that He will take "hold of your right hand" and "help you" (verse 13)? Why or why not?*

Day 7

Read Mark 15:42–46. *Why did it take courage for Joseph of Arimathea to ask Pilate for Jesus' body? How was Joseph's situation similar to Esther's? What do you learn from their examples?*

Week 38

GOD'S SUSTAINING POWER

Discover

Courage isn't a single moment of boldness; it's the quiet perseverance that happens over days, weeks, and even years. True courage is found in faithfully taking the next step . . . and the one after that . . . and then the one after that, even when obstacles are standing in the way.

God doesn't expect you to run the entire race at once. But He does want you to trust in Him to guide you each step forward. Furthermore, when life feels overwhelming, He says you can find refuge in His strength (see Psalm 91:9–10). He provides the courage to endure, step by step, so you can accomplish the purposes that He has set before you.

In this week's study, you will explore the perseverance of a man who thoroughly relied on God's sustaining power to help him lead the people of Israel through many challenges. In the process, you will discover how God offers you this same sustaining power today.

1. *How would you describe what it means to have perseverance?*

2. *What situation in your life requires perseverance right now?*

Experience

Trust Me, *and don't be afraid*. Many things feel out of control. Your routines are not running smoothly. You tend to feel more secure when your life is predictable. Let Me lead you to *the rock that is higher than you* and your circumstances. *Take refuge in the shelter of My wings*, where you are absolutely secure.

When you are shaken out of your comfortable routines, grip My hand tightly and look for growth opportunities. Instead of bemoaning the loss of your comfort, accept the challenge of something new. *I lead you on from glory to glory*, making you fit for My kingdom. Say *yes* to the ways I work in your life. Trust Me, and don't be afraid.

— From *Jesus Calling*, April 15

3. *"Many things feel out of control. Your routines are not running smoothly." How do you typically respond when your routines are upset? How do you want to respond?*

4. *"Take refuge in the shelter of My wings, where you are absolutely secure." How do you take shelter in God? What does it mean, in practice, to grip God's hand tightly?*

Dwell

Read Nehemiah 4:1–23. It is no stretch to say that you will "feel more secure when your life is predictable." The question is what you do when life is *un*predictable—when you are facing challenges like the people of God faced in this story. In spite of the looming threats from their enemies (led by Sanballat and Tobiah), the residents of Jerusalem pressed on in rebuilding the wall. Their remarkable courage stemmed from their trust in God's protection and guidance.

5. *What concerns did Sanballat have when he saw the work the Jewish people were doing? What did he and Tobiah initially try to do to discourage them (see verses 1–5)?*

6. *How did Nehemiah react when these enemies tried to shake up the people and physically disrupt the work they were doing to restore the walls?*

7. *Consider some of the ways this situation required courage from God's people. Where did Nehemiah's courage come from? Where did the builders' courage come from?*

8. *Have you been in a situation where you had to "build a wall" while being attacked? If so, where did you find the courage to overcome and continue on?*

Apply

The focus of this week's readings is on having the courage to persevere during frustrating or difficult times. Each day, read the passage slowly, pausing to reflect on what is being said. Remember, this is an opportunity to meet with God and tap into His sustaining power.

Day 1

Read 2 Chronicles 32:1–8. *What was the situation that King Hezekiah and the people of Judah were facing in this story? How is this situation similar to the situations you face today?*

Day 2

Read 2 Chronicles 32:9–14. *What reasons did Sennacherib give as to why the people of Judah should give up their courage? What did he say that was true? What did he say that was untrue?*

Day 3

Read 2 Chronicles 32:15–19. *Do you ever have a voice in your heart that says things like Sennacherib said? If so, how do you deal with that voice?*

Day 4

Read 2 Chronicles 32:20–22. *How important was Hezekiah's and the people's courage in the outcome of this conflict? What does this say about the importance of courage in your life?*

Day 5

Read Deuteronomy 20:1–2. *Why did Moses remind the people that God brought them out of Egypt? How does this message apply in your situation? What are the "horses and chariots" (verse 1) arrayed against you?*

Day 6

Read Deuteronomy 20:3–4. *Why do you suppose the Bible has so many passages that give the same reason for courage? What is God saying to His faithful followers?*

Day 7

Read Deuteronomy 20:5–8. *In what ways does other people's courage or cowardice affect you? How can your courage serve as a good influence to the people around you?*

Week 39

OVERCOMING FEAR

DISCOVER

Courage is essential to living out and sharing our faith. Many Christians around the world endure threats, violence, and persecution simply for practicing their faith in private. Their courage to stand firm in Christ, despite the consequences, is profoundly inspiring.

Even in societies where Christians are free to openly practice their faith, speaking about the gospel publicly can lead to rejection or tensions with family members, coworkers, and school systems. There is always the possibility of ridicule or isolation. This is why learning from the boldness of Jesus' first followers, as you will do this week, is so important.

The stories and examples of these early believers in Christ reveal how you can also be unafraid when it comes to speaking confidently about Jesus—and how you can do so in any setting. So, as you read their stories, consider how you can overcome fear in your life and depend on God's power to share the message of the gospel with courage and love.

1. *Think of a time you talked with a nonbeliever about Jesus. How courageous were you in expressing what you believe? What fears did you have to overcome?*

2. *What was the result of your conversation? If you could go back and do it over again, what would you change in your approach?*

Experience

Give yourself fully to the adventure of today. Walk boldly along the path of Life, relying on your ever-present Companion. You have every reason to be confident because My Presence accompanies you all the days of your life—and onward into eternity.

Do not give in to fear or worry, those robbers of abundant living. Trust Me enough to face problems as they come, rather than trying to anticipate them. *Fix your eyes on Me, the Author and Perfecter of your faith*, and many difficulties on the road ahead will vanish before you reach them. Whenever you start to feel afraid, remember that *I am holding you by your right hand*. Nothing can separate you from My Presence!

— From *Jesus Calling*, February 14

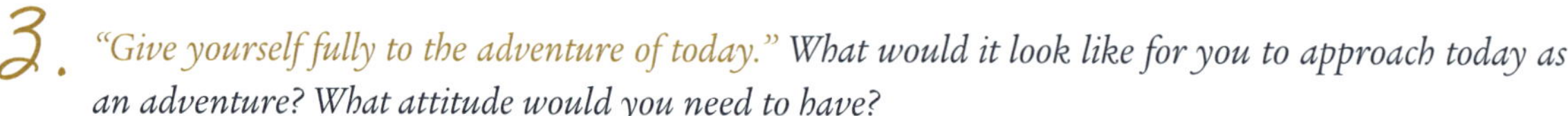

3. *"Give yourself fully to the adventure of today." What would it look like for you to approach today as an adventure? What attitude would you need to have?*

4. *"Do not give in to fear or worry, those robbers of abundant living." What are some of the ways fear or worry has robbed you of abundant living?*

Dwell

Read Acts 4:1–31 and reflect on the idea of walking "boldly along the path of Life." This story unfolds during a remarkable moment. Peter and John, filled with the Holy Spirit, boldly testify to the truth of what they have seen and experienced. They not only proclaim the message but also demonstrate the power of Christ by miraculously healing a lame beggar at the temple in Jerusalem, just as Jesus had done. Their act of healing draws a crowd, and Peter seizes the opportunity to share the message of Jesus. However, the disciples' testimony doesn't go unnoticed. Surrounded by religious authorities who could punish them, they stand courageously and continue to testify about Christ.

5. *Peter and John, in spite of the risks, decided to teach in the temple in Jerusalem. How did this demonstrate they were trusting in God "enough to face problems as they come"?*

6. *The Pharisees acknowledged that "everyone living in Jerusalem" (verse 16) knew about the healing of the paralyzed man. In what ways was this healing a problem for them?*

7. *In this case, the "difficulties on the road ahead" vanished in the immediate sense for Peter and John because the Jewish authorities released them. How did the members of the church react to the news? What did they ask God to give them (see verse 29)?*

8. *What are the risks of asking God to enable you to likewise speak His word "with great boldness" (verse 29)? What are the benefits of asking Him to do this?*

Apply

The focus of this week's readings is on having the courage to share your faith. Each day, read the passage slowly, pausing to reflect on what is being said. Remember, this is an opportunity to meet with Jesus and consider how you could more boldly proclaim His message of salvation.

Day 1

Read Acts 5:12–20. *What reasons do you have to be afraid when it comes to sharing your faith? What reasons do you have for being courageous?*

Day 2

Read Acts 5:21–28. *How did the apostles demonstrate courage after they had been thrown in jail? How did God protect them in this situation?*

Day 3

Read Acts 5:29–40. *How did Peter demonstrate courage before the Sanhedrin? How would being flogged/ beaten have likely affected your willingness to proclaim the gospel?*

Day 4

Read Acts 5:41–42. *Could you rejoice for being counted worthy to suffer disgrace for Jesus' sake? What would make this especially difficult for you to do?*

Day 5

Read Acts 6:8–15. *Given what has happened up to this point in Acts, would you expect Stephen to be protected from harm? Why or why not?*

Day 6

Read Acts 7:54–59. *Why do you think God didn't protect Stephen the way He had protected Peter and John earlier?*

Day 7

Read Acts 7:60. *Would you expect Stephen's fate to make the believers more afraid of speaking up about Jesus? Why or why not? How does Stephen's story inspire you to witness for Jesus?*

Week 40

WALKING IN VICTORY

Discover

Anytime fear begins to creep in, it is important to remind yourself to trust in God's power and protection. Do this first, before you do anything else.

Scripture warns that Satan, your enemy, "prowls around like a roaring lion looking for someone to devour" (1 Peter 5:8). Like any predator, he looks for moments of weakness, trying to invoke fear and separate you from the closeness you share with Jesus and with other believers. But take heart. Although the enemy is powerful, God is infinitely greater.

By fitting you with His own armor and equipping you with spiritual weapons and wisdom, He ensures that you can stand firm in Christ's strength and boldly resist any deception or attack from the enemy. In this session, you will explore how to put on these spiritual armaments to overcome fear, find courage in Christ, and walk in victory.

1. *What comes to mind when you picture Satan as a roaring lion who is looking for someone to devour? What fears, if any, does that create in you?*

2. *In the Bible, God is also depicted as a lion—the Lion of Judah who protects His people. What difference should this make for you when you're face to face with the enemy?*

Experience

Trust Me, *and don't be afraid.* I want you to view trials as exercises designed to develop your trust-muscles. You live in the midst of fierce spiritual battles, and fear is one of Satan's favorite weapons. When you start to feel afraid, affirm your trust in Me. Speak out loud, if circumstances permit. *Resist the devil in My Name, and he will slink away from you.* Refresh yourself in My holy Presence. Speak or sing praises to Me, and My Face will shine radiantly upon you.

Remember that *there is no condemnation for those who belong to Me.* You have been judged NOT GUILTY for all eternity. *Trust Me, and don't be afraid; for I am your Strength, Song, and Salvation.*

– From *Jesus Calling*, August 22

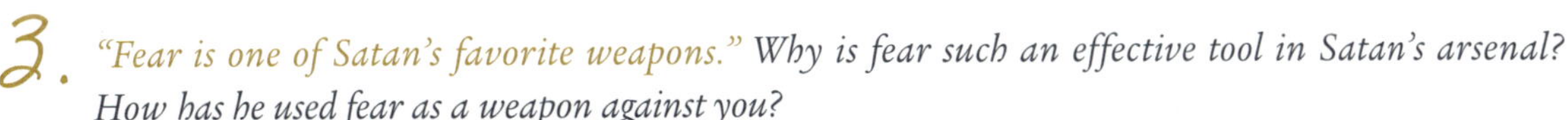

3. *"Fear is one of Satan's favorite weapons." Why is fear such an effective tool in Satan's arsenal? How has he used fear as a weapon against you?*

4. *"Resist the devil." James writes, "Resist the devil, and he will flee from you" (4:7 NKJV). How do you actively resist Satan when he attacks you with fear?*

Dwell

Read Ephesians 6:10–20. The Bible is clear that "you live in the midst of fierce spiritual battles." For this reason, you need a way to protect yourself from the enemy's attacks—and a way to fight back. In this passage, Paul uses the allegory of a Roman soldier's basic equipment to show the spiritual "armor" and "weapon" that God has provided to help you stand strong in Him. This equipment includes the belt of truth, the breastplate of righteousness, the shoes of peace, the shield of faith, the helmet of salvation, and the sword of the Spirit (God's Word). Paul also emphasizes the importance of prayer and perseverance during trials.

5. *How does Paul describe the nature of the "fierce spiritual battles" that are being waged around you? How does he describe the nature of your enemy?*

6. *As you read this passage, why do you think Paul focuses more on your ability to stand firm against the enemy than on going on the offensive and trying to attack the enemy?*

7. *What do you learn about the power of prayer—communication with your "Commander"—in verses 18–20? How does prayer enable you to stand strong against your enemy?*

8. *How can knowing you have this spiritual equipment available to you help you "view trials as exercises designed to develop your trust-muscles" in the Lord?*

Apply

The focus of this week's readings is on what it means to walk in the victory that Jesus has provided. Each day, read the passage slowly, pausing to consider what is being said. Remember, this is an opportunity to meet with Jesus and learn what it means to truly follow Him.

Day 1

Read Matthew 4:18–22. *What have you given up in your life to follow Jesus? What victories have you gained by following Christ?*

Day 2

Read James 1:5–8. *Do you ever doubt the path that Jesus has set for you? Do you ever doubt that He has given you the victory? If so, how do you deal with these doubts?*

Day 3

Read James 1:5–8 again. *How can believers in Christ help each other deal with doubts?*

Day 4

Read Acts 9:10–19. *When have you witnessed someone acting courageously for Christ? How does it impact you to learn about Christians who take such big risks?*

Day 5

Read Acts 9:20–25. *In what ways are you reluctant to speak up about your decision to follow Jesus? In which situations do you fear rejection?*

Day 6

Read Acts 9:26–31. *How does Paul's story ignite your courage to share the gospel with others?*

Day 7

Read Acts 12:1–11. *In this account, what do the fates of the disciples James and Peter teach you about the cost that is involved in following Jesus?*

Week 41

THE GATEWAY TO PEACE

Discover

If there's one thing we yearn for deep in our hearts, it's peace. More than just a fleeting feeling, true peace gives us a sense of stability and well-being even in the middle of life's storms.

The Bible teaches that peace is the result of a strong relationship with God. This begins with accepting the peace Jesus offers. He took the first step, paving the way for us to experience harmony with God. When we place our trust in Him, we are gifted a profound peace independent of life's circumstances.

Faith in Christ is the gateway to this peace. Trusting God doesn't guarantee the absence of storms, but it does provide the assurance that we are not alone. In this session, we look at where true peace comes from and some of the ways God uses it in our lives.

1. *How peaceful was your childhood? To what do you attribute that?*

2. *How peaceful is your life now? To what do you attribute that?*

Experience

MY PEACE is the treasure of treasures: *the pearl of great price*. It is an exquisitely costly gift, both for the Giver and the receiver. I purchased this Peace for you with My blood. You receive this gift by trusting Me in the midst of life's storms. If you have the world's peace—everything going your way—you don't seek My unfathomable Peace. Thank Me when things do not go your way, because spiritual blessings come wrapped in trials. Adverse circumstances are normal in a fallen world. Expect them each day. Rejoice in the face of hardship, *for I have overcome the world.*

– From *Jesus Calling*, January 24

3. *"My Peace is the treasure of treasures . . . an exquisitely costly gift." What does it mean that Jesus purchased His peace for you with His blood? Why was this even necessary?*

4. *"Adverse circumstances are normal in a fallen world." Do you tend to think of adverse circumstances as normal—what anyone can expect as a part of life on this earth—or as surprises and outrages? Why did you answer the way you did?*

Dwell

Read Romans 5:1–2, 6–11. In these verses, Paul discusses the blessings that we, as followers of Jesus, receive because we have been "justified through faith" (verse 1). The term *justify* means that God has declared us righteous and no longer subject to His divine wrath. This imputed righteousness is not based on our merit but on the merit of Jesus' sacrifice for our sins—which we receive by faith. As Paul wrote, one of the blessings we receive because of justification is God's peace—truly the "treasure of treasures" and "the pearl of great price."

5. *What does it mean that "we have been justified through faith" (verse 1)? What role does faith in Jesus play in restoring a relationship of peace with God?*

6. *Jesus purchased our peace with God with His blood. How does Paul describe our state when Christ determined to die for us (see verses 6–8)?*

7. *What are the results of our being "justified by [Jesus'] blood" (verse 9)? What peace do we now possess because Christ has reconciled us with God?*

8. *How have you experienced peace with God? What is it like for you? If you haven't experienced it, what is the lack of peace with Him like for you?*

Apply

The focus of this week's readings is on receiving God's peace. Each day, read the passage slowly, pausing to think about what is being said and the truths that are being shared. Remember, this is an opportunity to meet with Jesus and receive His peace.

Day 1

Read Numbers 6:23–26. *Why is it important to know that peace is a blessing that God offers to His children—not something that you can devise by your own efforts?*

Day 2

Read Psalm 4:6–8. *What is the psalmist's prayer to the Lord in this passage? What does he say about the kind of peace that God has provided?*

Day 3

Read Psalm 29:3–9. *How does the psalmist portray the Lord in these verses? How do you respond to this picture of God?*

Day 4

Read Psalm 29:10–11. *What is your response to the psalmist's statement that the all-powerful and mighty Lord God blesses His people with peace? How does this reassure you?*

Day 5

Read Psalm 34:12–16. *What must you do if you want "to see many good days" (verse 12)? What are you to seek and pursue?*

Day 6

Read 1 Peter 3:8–12. *Peter echoes Psalm 34:12–16 in this passage, urging believers in Christ to pursue peace. How do you go about pursuing peace with God and others?*

Day 7

Read Psalm 85:8–9. *Here again we see the fear of the Lord in the same passage as a promise of peace. How does fearing the Lord enable you to gain His peace? What is the connection?*

Week 42

TRUST AND OBEY

Discover

True peace is not found in the world around us, nor in circumstances, human relationships, or even wealth and earthly comforts. Instead, it comes through trusting in the Lord. When we trust Him, we can stop striving and rest in His care.

An old hymn proclaims, "When we walk with the Lord in the light of His Word, what a glory He sheds on our way. While we do His good will, He abides with us still, and with all who will trust and obey." There is a connection between peace and trusting and obeying God. When we entrust our lives to Him, and then demonstrate that trust by obeying His will, we find that He leads us "beside quiet waters" and "refreshes [our] soul" (Psalm 23:2–3).

This week you will see how integral Jesus is in the connection between love, trust, and peace—as well as the role your own obedience plays.

1. *When you were a child, how inclined were you to obey your parents? Did you tend to be compliant or were you strong-willed? Explain your response.*

2. *Would you describe your parents as strong disciplinarians or more permissive? What are some reasons for answering as you did?*

Experience

Learn to live from your true Center in Me. I reside in the deepest depths of your being, in eternal union with your spirit. It is at this deep level that My Peace reigns continually. You will not find lasting peace in the world around you, in circumstances, or in human relationships. The external world is always in flux—under the curse of death and decay. But there is a gold mine of Peace deep within you, waiting to be tapped. Take time to delve into the riches of My residing Presence. I want you to live increasingly from your real Center, where My Love has an eternal grip on you. *I am Christ in you, the hope of Glory.*

— From *Jesus Calling*, February 20

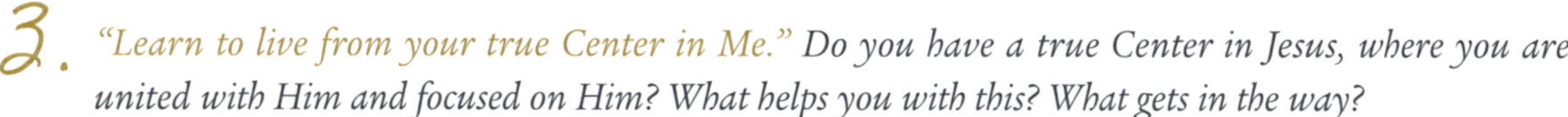

3. *"Learn to live from your true Center in Me." Do you have a true Center in Jesus, where you are united with Him and focused on Him? What helps you with this? What gets in the way?*

4. *"You will not find lasting peace in the world around you, in circumstances, or in human relationships." In what ways have you found this to be true? Why do you think that lasting peace cannot be found in anything that the world offers?*

DWELL

Read John 14:23–27. Jesus reassures His disciples in this passage, promising them the Presence of the Holy Spirit after His departure. This indwelling of the Holy Spirit would serve as "a gold mine of Peace . . . waiting to be tapped." Furthermore, this peace would not be like the world's peace. It would be a gift of all-surpassing comfort and courage that came from God alone (see Philippians 4:7).

5. *Jesus says, "Anyone who loves me will obey my teaching" (verse 23). Why does love have this effect? How would you describe the link between love and obedience?*

6. *Jesus states the inverse is also true: "Anyone who does not love me will not obey my teaching" (verse 24). How does your obedience to Christ demonstrate your love for Him?*

7. *Jesus told His disciples the Holy Spirit would "reside in the deepest depths of [their] being." In what ways would the Holy Spirit help them after He had departed from their midst?*

8. *What else do you learn about the peace of God in this passage? What does it mean that Jesus does not give this peace to you "as the world gives" (verse 27)?*

Apply

The focus of this week's readings is on developing the kind of obedience that leads to peace. Each day, read the passage slowly, pausing to reflect on what is being said. Remember, this is an opportunity to meet with Jesus and demonstrate your obedience to Him.

Day 1

Read Psalm 103:17–20. *In what particular area of your life is God calling you to obedience? How is He guiding you in your current situation?*

Day 2

Read Psalm 119:33–35. *Why is it important to obey with all your heart—not grudgingly?*

Day 3

Read Psalm 119:33–35 again. *How can you see yourself finding peace by following God's guidance for you today?*

Day 4

Read Matthew 28:18–20. *Jesus gave this command (called the Great Commission) to His followers just before He ascended into heaven after His resurrection. What does Jesus promise in this passage? What does He require of His disciples?*

Day 5

Read Matthew 28:18–20 again. *How are you actively heeding this command from Jesus today? What are some things, if any, that have gotten in the way?*

Day 6

Read Luke 11:27–28. *Does it surprise you that Jesus attached a blessing to hearing and obeying the Word of God rather than to something else (like believing)? Explain.*

Day 7

Read Romans 6:16–18. *How does a person move from being a "[slave] to sin" (verse 16) to being a "[slave] to righteousness" (verse 18)? What role does obedience to God play in the process?*

Week 43

THE SPIRIT'S PEACE

DISCOVER

While we resonate with the humanity of Jesus and His sacrifice for us, the presence and work of the Holy Spirit is often less understood. Yet the Bible is clear that the Holy Spirit is our Advocate and Helper (see John 14:16, 26), divinely sent to empower us to lead lives of wisdom, love, faith, and obedience. By getting to know and better understand who the Holy Spirit is, we also open our hearts to the peace that comes from His presence.

When you accepted Jesus as your Savior, the Holy Spirit came to dwell within you, offering you the same closeness as Jesus did when He walked among His disciples. As Paul wrote, you became "God's temple and . . . God's Spirit dwells in your midst" (1 Corinthians 3:16). Given this reality—that the Holy Spirit "lives with you and will be in you" (John 14:17)—it is important to learn as much as you can about Him!

This is what you will be invited to do in this week's study. You will reflect on the Holy Spirit's vital role in your life and how His presence roots you deeply in God's peace.

1. *What are your perceptions of the Holy Spirit? How do you tend to view Him?*

2. *What has brought you peace or a lack of peace in your day today?*

Experience

UNDERSTANDING will never bring you Peace. That's why I have instructed you to *trust in Me, not in your understanding*. Human beings have a voracious appetite for trying to figure things out in order to gain a sense of mastery over their lives. But the world presents you with an endless series of problems. As soon as you master one set, another pops up to challenge you. The relief you had anticipated is short-lived. Soon your mind is gearing up again: searching for understanding (mastery) instead of seeking Me (your Master).

The wisest of all men, Solomon, could never think his way through to Peace. His vast understanding resulted in feelings of futility rather than in fulfillment. Finally, he lost his way and succumbed to the will of his wives by worshiping idols.

My Peace is not an elusive goal, hidden at the center of some complicated maze. Actually, you are always enveloped in Peace, which is inherent in My Presence. As you look to Me, you gain awareness of this precious Peace.

— From *Jesus Calling*, August 7

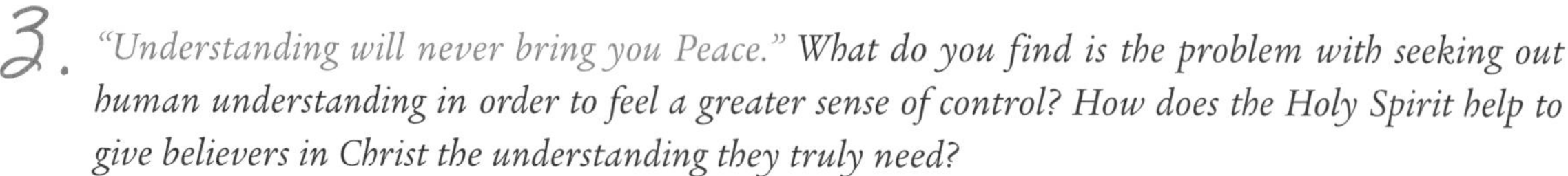

3. "Understanding will never bring you Peace." *What do you find is the problem with seeking out human understanding in order to feel a greater sense of control? How does the Holy Spirit help to give believers in Christ the understanding they truly need?*

4. *"You are always enveloped in Peace, which is inherent in My Presence." Paul writes that peace is a fruit of the Spirit (see Galatians 5:22). How does the Holy Spirit make believers aware of Jesus' precious peace? What is your role, as a Christian, in seeking that peace?*

DWELL

Read Romans 8:5–11. In these verses, Paul draws attention to two ways your mind can be focused: (1) on the desires of the flesh or (2) on the desires of the Holy Spirit. While Paul uses the term *flesh*, he isn't simply referring to your body or purely sinful actions. Instead, he describes a mindset that ignores Jesus and the Holy Spirit and focuses solely on self-centered concerns—in other words, a mindset that is "searching for understanding (mastery) instead of seeking [God] (your Master)." The closer you align your thoughts with the Holy Spirit, the more deeply you will experience God's peace, even in the midst of life's challenges.

5. *How does Paul describe a person whose mind is "governed by the flesh" (verse 6)? What are the traits of a person whose mind is "set on what the Spirit desires" (verse 5)?*

6. *Given these two different mindsets, why do you think life and peace come only to those who set their hearts on the things the Spirit desires?*

7. *How would you define what it means that "the Spirit of God lives in you" (verse 9)? Why do you think this is a determining factor as to whether someone belongs to Christ?*

8. *You are "always enveloped in [God's] Peace" if you belong to Christ. What peace does Paul say you have regarding your eternal security if you belong to Jesus?*

Apply

The focus of this week's readings is on receiving peace through the work of the Holy Spirit in your life. Each day, read the passage slowly, pausing to focus on what is being said. Remember, this is an opportunity to meet with Jesus and learn how the Holy Spirit is at work in your life.

Day 1

Read Galatians 5:13–15. *What do you think Paul means when says not to "bite and devour each other" (verse 15)? How does godly discipline help you to live in peace with others?*

Day 2

Read Galatians 5:16–18. *What is a fleshly desire that you need to put aside in order to live in the peace that the Holy Spirit offers?*

Day 3

Read Galatians 5:19–21. *How do the acts of the flesh lead away from peace? What warning does Paul give for those who choose to live this way?*

Day 4

Read Galatians 5:22–23. *Why do you think Paul calls the traits he describes "fruit of the Spirit" (verse 22)? What does calling them fruit tell you about these characteristics?*

Day 5

Read Galatians 5:22–23 again. *Where do you see the fruit of peace in the lives of Christians you know? Where do you see the fruit of the Spirit in your life? In what areas do you need to grow?*

Day 6

Read Galatians 5:24–26. *Paul previously emphasized the need to "walk by the spirit" (verse 16), but here he stresses you are also to "keep in step with the Spirit" (verse 25). Why do you think Paul places such importance on "walking" and "keeping in step" with the Spirit's work?*

Day 7

Reread all of Galatians 5:16–26. *What have you learned about the connection between the Holy Spirit and peace? What about the connection between the flesh and a lack of peace?*

Week 44
PEACE IN ADVERSITY

Discover

It's easy to feel at peace when life is running smoothly. But what about when everything falls apart? When tragedy erupts or a loved one is diagnosed with a terminal illness? When you lose your job and the future suddenly feels full of uncertainty?

As counterintuitive as it may seem, there is peace to be found during such times. Jesus promised, "Surely I am with you always, to the very end of the age" (Matthew 28:20). He also said, "I will not leave you as orphans; I will come to you" (John 14:18). Jesus promises to never leave you, no matter what you face. When you trust these promises, your faith grows stronger and your peace becomes more resilient—tested and refined like gold in the fire.

In this week's study, you will explore the story of a faithful man in the Bible who experienced profound suffering yet determined to lean on God through it all. After considering his experience, you will reflect on some of your own challenges and discover how you can have more of God's unshakable peace even in the face of adversity.

1. *When you were growing up, how did your parents cope with hard times?*

2. *Why is it often difficult for even Christians to feel God's presence during times of suffering?*

Experience

RECEIVE MY PEACE. It is My continual gift to you. The best way to receive this gift is to sit quietly in My Presence, trusting Me in every area of your life. *Quietness and trust* accomplish far more than you can imagine: not only in you, but also on earth and in heaven. When you trust Me in a given area, you release that problem or person into My care.

Spending time alone with Me can be a difficult discipline because it goes against the activity addiction of this age. You may appear to be doing nothing, but actually you are participating in battles going on within spiritual realms. You are waging war—not with *the weapons of the world*, but with heavenly weapons, which *have divine power to demolish strongholds*. Living close to Me is a sure defense against evil.

— From *Jesus Calling*, September 12

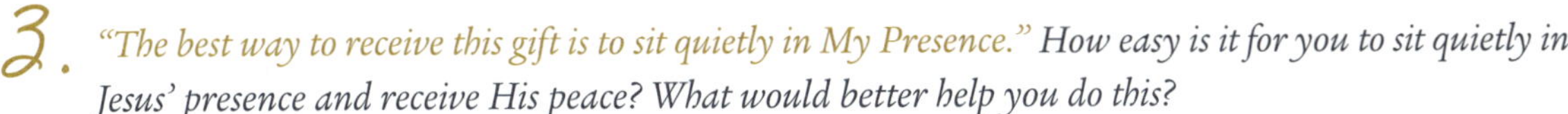

3. *"The best way to receive this gift is to sit quietly in My Presence." How easy is it for you to sit quietly in Jesus' presence and receive His peace? What would better help you do this?*

4. *"Quietness and trust accomplish far more than you can imagine . . . on earth and in heaven." How do you respond to this idea that your quietness and trust in God could actually accomplish something in the spiritual realm? In what ways could this be true?*

Dwell

Read Job 1:1–22. The story of Job is about grappling with the unexpected ways that God's plans often unfold. It reveals that suffering is not always a direct result of sin but is always a part of the human experience in a fallen world—and that you can choose to trust "[God] in every area of your life" regardless of what comes. Ultimately, even when life feels overwhelming or unfair, you can rest in God's wisdom and sovereignty, knowing His understanding far surpasses your own and His grace and Presence will accompany you through the fire and the flood.

5. *How does the author of this story make it clear that Job was a righteous man? Given this, do you think God betrayed Job by letting Satan test him? Why or why not?*

6. *Job did not realize he was "participating in battles going on within spiritual realms." What do you think was God's ultimate purpose in allowing Satan to test him?*

7. *Consider Job's response in verses 20–22 to the tragic news he receives. What feelings and beliefs does he express? What did he* not *do in response to this crisis in his life?*

8. *What do you learn from this story about one possible reason why God might allow suffering? What do you learn from Job's example about how to respond to it?*

Apply

The focus of this week's readings is on having peace in the midst of trials. Each day, read the passage slowly, considering the truths being presented. Remember, this is an opportunity to meet with Jesus and seek His peace in the midst of the adversity you are facing.

Day 1

Read Isaiah 30:19–21. *These verses come after God rebukes the people of Judah for trusting in a military alliance with Egypt for protection—an act of rebellion and a sign of their lack of faith. What does God know about their situation? What does He promise to do to aid them?*

Day 2

Read Isaiah 26:3–4. *Trust is key. What are some reasons you have for trusting in the Lord?*

Day 3

Read Isaiah 32:16–17. *Why do you suppose righteousness leads to peace for the people of God? What are some ways that you cultivate righteousness in your own life?*

Day 4

Read Isaiah 32:18–20. *Does it seem like you are living in a place where "hail flattens" and "the city is leveled completely" (verse 19)? What promise is found in this passage?*

Day 5

Read Isaiah 53:4–6. *This Old Testament prophecy tells of what Jesus will do for His followers. What has Christ done with your sufferings? How aware of this are you?*

Day 6

Read Isaiah 54:10–12. *Here the Lord is talking to Jerusalem, the capital city of His people, which had been demolished because of the people's sin. What does He promise His people in verse 10? What other aspects of His promises in this passage are especially meaningful to you—and why?*

Day 7

Read Isaiah 54:13–15. *The Lord made these promises to His people, yet history reveals that their circumstances didn't necessarily get better quickly. What do you draw from this? Why would God make promises like these and then require His people to wait to see them fulfilled?*

Week 45

PEACE WITH OTHERS

Discover

Living at peace with others is a central theme in the Bible. In fact, Scripture calls you to pursue harmony and work toward it—especially with fellow believers. Through Jesus' sacrifice on the cross, you are not only reconciled with God but are also able to reconcile with others.

Jesus said to His followers, "A new commandment I give to you, that you love one another; as I have loved you, that you also love one another" (John 13:34 NKJV). When Jesus made you a new creation, He also called you to tear down any walls that stand between you and others. True love and peace become possible when you open your heart to this command.

This week's study is about living at peace with others. As you prepare for it, think about your own relationships, especially any that feel strained or broken. Consider how Jesus can work through you to bring healing and restore wholeness. Division should never define your interactions. Through Christ, unity and love can transform how you relate to others.

1. *When you disagree with someone, what is your typical means of dealing with it? Are you inclined to argue, withdraw, talk it through calmly, or pretend nothing is wrong? Explain.*

2. *If you are a believer in Jesus, what is something you would like to change as it relates to how you get along with your fellow brothers and sisters in Christ?*

Experience

COME TO ME, and rest in My Peace. My Face is shining upon you, in rays of *Peace transcending understanding*. Instead of trying to figure things out yourself, you can relax in the Presence of the One who knows everything. As you lean on Me in trusting dependence, you feel peaceful and complete. This is how I designed you to live: in close communion with Me.

When you are around other people, you tend to cater to their expectations—real or imagined. You feel enslaved to pleasing them, and your awareness of My Presence grows dim. Your efforts to win their approval eventually exhaust you. You offer these people dry crumbs rather than the *living water* of My Spirit flowing through you. This is not My way for you! Stay in touch with Me, even during your busiest moments. Let My Spirit give you words of grace as you live in the Light of My Peace.

– From *Jesus Calling*, November 18

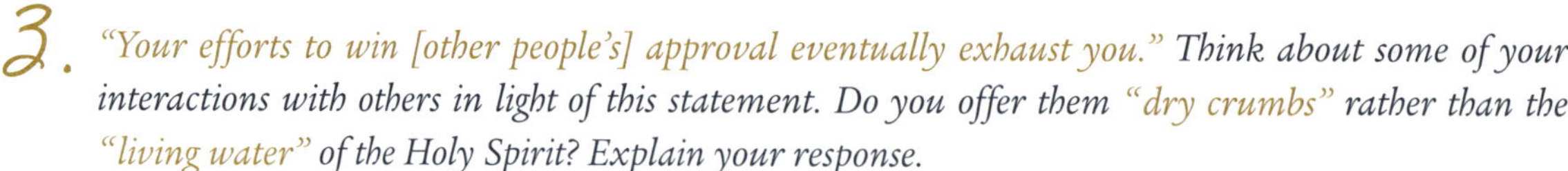

3. *"Your efforts to win [other people's] approval eventually exhaust you." Think about some of your interactions with others in light of this statement. Do you offer them "dry crumbs" rather than the "living water" of the Holy Spirit? Explain your response.*

4. *"Stay in touch with Me, even during your busiest moments." What are some ways you stay in touch with Jesus during your busiest moments and speak His words of grace to others?*

DWELL

Read Ephesians 2:11–22. Paul's message in these verses provides an overview of how you are to treat your fellow brothers and sisters in Christ—offering them not "dry crumbs" but the very "living water of [God's] Spirit flowing through you." In this, Paul emphasizes the need for unity, reconciliation, and the breaking down of barriers between different groups.

5. *What reminder does Paul give at the start of this passage to those who are "Gentiles by birth" (verse 11)? From what were they once excluded?*

6. *What difference does it make that Jesus "destroyed the barrier" (verse 14) between people, making it possible for all—regardless of their ethnic background—to live in peace?*

7. *What example of peace did Jesus set for His followers—both Jews and Gentiles alike? Why is it important that Jesus left this model for peace for the church?*

8. *Paul wanted believers to think of themselves as stones being put together into a single temple of the Lord. How does this image motivate you to seek peace with those you've been avoiding or find it hard to get along with? What is one step you could take toward peace?*

Apply

The focus of this week's readings is on the peace God desires you to have and to extend to others. Each day, read the passage slowly, removing all distractions to concentrate on what is being said. Remember, this is an opportunity to meet with Jesus and abide in His peace.

Day 1

Read Colossians 1:15–16. *Thrones, powers, rulers, and authorities refer to angelic powers (and possibly earthly ones as well). What does this say about Jesus' authority over this world?*

Day 2

Read Colossians 1:17. *How does it bring you peace to know that Jesus holds all things together?*

Day 3

Read Colossians 1:18. *Jesus' authority extends to His body—the church. How should this reality affect the relationships you have with those in His church?*

Day 4

Read Colossians 1:19–20. *What does Paul say about how God has reconciled all things to Himself? What was the price involved for God to make peace with you?*

Day 5

Read Colossians 1:21–22. *How does Paul describe your relationship to God before you accepted Christ? In what ways do you identify with the description of your past in these verses?*

Day 6

Read Colossians 1:22–23. *What has God done for you and for every other believer through Jesus? What does this have to do with your peace? What does this say about living at peace with your fellow brothers and sisters in Christ?*

Day 7

Read all of Colossians 1:15–23. *When you consider this passage as a whole, what is God asking His people to do? What will that look like for you today?*

Week 46

PEACE THAT EMPOWERS

Discover

Society often advertises that peace can be found in worldly things. It promises that wealth will lead to security, that relationships will lead to happiness, and that status will lead to contentment. However, the Bible points to a far different source when it comes to peace.

The apostle Paul wrote about this source in his letter to the believers in Philippi. He did so not from a place of comfort but from a prison cell, where he was facing the possibility of being executed for proclaiming the gospel. Meanwhile, the small group of believers to whom he was writing was facing many challenges of their own, as their city was hostile to the gospel. Following Christ in their circumstances was anything but simple!

In this week's study, you will see that Paul didn't promise the believers in Philippi a trouble-free life. Rather, he proclaimed the kind of peace we all need—not one that erases challenges but one that, through trust in God, empowers us to face hardship with hope and resilience.

1. *What messages have you received from the world about what brings true peace? Give some specific examples.*

2. *What are some things you do to find peace? What do you tend to focus on when you need peace?*

Experience

My Face is shining upon you, beaming out *Peace that transcends understanding*. You are surrounded by a sea of problems, but you are face-to-Face with Me, your Peace. As long as you focus on Me, you are safe. If you gaze too long at the myriad problems around you, you will sink under the weight of your burdens. When you start to sink, simply call out, "Help me, Jesus!" and I will lift you up.

The closer you live to Me, the safer you are. Circumstances around you are undulating, and there are treacherous-looking waves in the distance. *Fix your eyes on Me*, the One who never changes. By the time those waves reach you, they will have shrunk to proportions of My design. I am always beside you, helping you face *today's* waves. The future is a phantom, seeking to spook you. Laugh at the future! Stay close to Me.

– From *Jesus Calling*, January 15

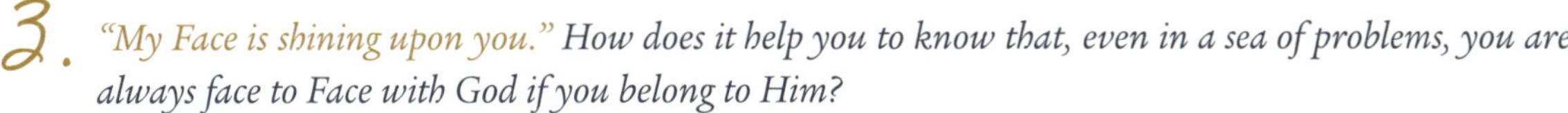

3. *"My Face is shining upon you." How does it help you to know that, even in a sea of problems, you are always face to Face with God if you belong to Him?*

4. *"Circumstances around you are undulating, and there are treacherous-looking waves in the distance." What are some things God calls His children to do to deal with their problems?*

DWELL

Read Philippians 4:4–13. Paul was no stranger to being "surrounded by a sea of problems." Yet even in jail, he could find a peace and joy that transcended his circumstances. Writing to the believers in Philippi, who were likely troubled by news of his imprisonment, he reminded them of a powerful truth: Real peace comes from trusting in God and relying on His strength. His letter encouraged the Philippians (and us today) to follow his example, cultivating a life rooted in God where peace is not dependent on external events but on an abiding faith in Him.

5. *The believers in Philippi were undergoing discrimination because of their faith. In spite of this, what did Paul instruct them to do (see verses 4–5)?*

6. *Gazing too long "at the myriad problems around you" will only lead to anxiety and despair. What alternate course does Paul advise? Where does that course of action lead?*

7. *What is the further benefit of focusing your mind on things that are noble, right, pure, lovely, admirable, excellent, and praiseworthy when you are faced with trials?*

8. *What "secret" (verse 12) had Paul learned that enabled him to be content in every situation? How had he learned to fix his eyes on "the One who never changes"?*

APPLY

The focus of this week's readings is on laying hold of the peace that is found in trusting God and relying on His strength. Each day, read the passage slowly, pausing to think about what is being said. Remember, this is an opportunity to meet with Jesus and draw from His strength.

Day 1

Read Romans 15:13. *What is the connection between hope and peace? What is the connection between trust in God and peace?*

Day 2

Read John 16:33. *Jesus said, "In this world you will have trouble." What trouble are you dealing with today? How can you have peace despite that trouble?*

Day 3

Read John 20:19. *"Peace be with you!" was the normal way of saying hello in the culture of that day. But what additional meaning do the circumstances of this scene give to these words—which Jesus said right after His crucifixion and resurrection?*

Day 4

Read John 20:20. *Why do you think Jesus showed His disciples the nail wounds in His hands and the spear wound in His side? How do those contribute to your peace?*

Day 5

Read John 20:21. *Jesus again says, "Peace be with you!" How does peace connect with Jesus' next statement: "As the Father has sent me, I am sending you"?*

Day 6

Read Proverbs 3:1–4. *Which actions open the way for you to experience God's peace and prosperity? What is the connection?*

Day 7

Read Proverbs 3:13–18. *How can you cultivate wisdom? In what ways have you seen godly wisdom lead you on the "paths" of peace (verse 17)?*

Week 47

INHERITING PEACE

Discover

When you hear the word *inheritance*, what comes to mind? Maybe you picture a person receiving something meaningful from a loved one who has passed away, as expressed in a written will that ensures possessions are entrusted to the designated heirs.

Similarly, God has lovingly prepared an eternal inheritance, detailed in the pages of His Word, that He has designated for each member of His spiritual family. Those who accept Jesus are God's rightful heirs, and He offers them the unmerited, unfathomable gift of eternal life. Once you begin to grasp the certainty of this divine promise, you gain a deepening sense of peace that remains regardless of the challenges confronting you or the chaos surrounding you.

In this week's study, you will explore truths that confirm your inheritance in Christ, anchor you in this hope, and provide you with an assurance of peace.

1. *What is one thing (if any) that has been left to you as part of an inheritance? What are some things you would like to leave to your children or loved ones?*

2. *When you were a child, what did your parents do that let you know you were secure in their love? Or what did they do that left you feeling insecure?*

Experience

You are Mine for all time—and beyond time, into eternity. No power can deny you your inheritance in heaven. I want you to realize how utterly secure you are! Even if you falter as you journey through life, I will never let go of your hand.

Knowing that your future is absolutely assured can free you to live abundantly today. I have prepared this day for you with the most tender concern and attention to detail. Instead of approaching the day as a blank page that you need to fill up, try living it in a responsive mode, being on the lookout for all that I am doing. This sounds easy, but it requires a deep level of trust, based on the knowledge that *My way is perfect.*

– From *Jesus Calling*, March 10

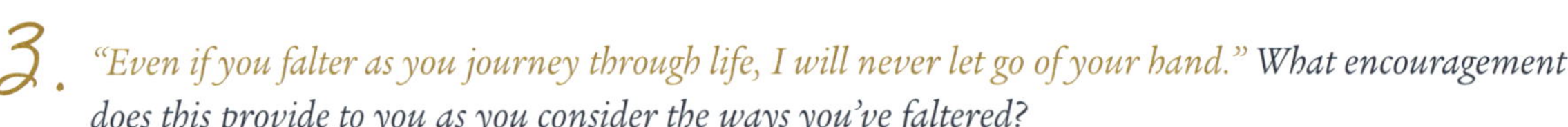

3. *"Even if you falter as you journey through life, I will never let go of your hand." What encouragement does this provide to you as you consider the ways you've faltered?*

4. *"Knowing that your future is absolutely assured can free you to live abundantly today." How does the fact you have an inheritance in heaven allow you to live abundantly today?*

Dwell

Read Colossians 3:12–17, 23–25. In this passage, Paul advises you to "clothe" or "put on" (NKJV) certain characteristics that identify you as a member of God's chosen people. These are traits that show the world you belong to God "for all time—and beyond time, into eternity," and as you put them on, you allow "the peace of Christ" (verse 15) to rule in your heart. These characteristics, Paul notes, should relate to *all* aspects of your life.

5. *What do traits such as compassion, kindness, humility, gentleness, and patience communicate to people? How do these traits foster peace between people?*

6. *Why does Paul stress the need for followers of Jesus to "bear with each other and forgive one another" (verse 13)? How does this lead to abundant living?*

7. *Why is it critical to allow the peace of Christ to "rule" in your heart (verse 15)? How will it impact the way you treat others if the peace of Jesus is truly ruling in your heart?*

8. *What does it mean to do "whatever you do" as if you were "working for the Lord" (verse 23)? How should this impact the way you live at peace with others?*

Apply

The focus of this week's readings is on the peace that comes from knowing God has reserved an eternal inheritance for you. Each day, read the passage slowly, pausing to reflect on what is being said and the truths that are being revealed to you. Remember, this is an opportunity to meet with Jesus and learn about the eternal inheritance you have received through Him.

Day 1

Read Ephesians 1:3–4. *For what goal did God choose you to be His child? How is it possible for you as a Christian to be blameless in His sight?*

Day 2

Read Ephesians 1:5–6. *When Paul refers to "adoption to sonship" (verse 5), it means that, through Christ, you have been given the full legal rights of adult heirs. (Paul was thinking here of Roman law.) What do heirs of God possess? How does this matter to you?*

Day 3

Read Ephesians 1:7–10. *You have received redemption, "the forgiveness of sins" (verse 7), through Christ's blood. How does that impact your view of sin and its consequences?*

Day 4

Read Ephesians 1:11–12. *God works out everything according to His will for His children. This means your life of faith will bring glory to Jesus, even if you don't think you're doing anything remarkable. How does that assurance affect the way you see yourself?*

Day 5

Read 1 Peter 2:4–5. *If you are a Christian, you are like one of the stones being built together into a spiritual house (or a temple of the Holy Spirit). How should that impact the way you see yourself? How should it affect the way you live?*

Day 6

Read 1 Peter 2:6. *What is the promise in this verse? How does that promise give you peace as a believer in Christ to face whatever comes your way?*

Day 7

Read 1 Peter 2:9–10. *Why are these descriptions—a chosen people, a royal priesthood, a holy nation—significant not just for you as an individual but also for you as part of a group?*

Week 48

SHAPED BY DISCIPLINE

Discover

There's a reason why discipline isn't a popular topic. Discipline can feel restrictive, which is the opposite of the personal autonomy we so highly value as humans. However, if left to ourselves, we are prone to chase things that ultimately harm or distract us.

Truthfully, *these* are the things that restrict us from the good that God has in store for us. Divine discipline, on the other hand, is capable of producing the kind of freedom that sets us free from the bondage of negative habits and unhelpful tendencies.

This week you will explore how God uses challenges and hardships to shape you into the person He created you to be. While discipline isn't easy or pleasant, your loving heavenly Father uses it to nurture spiritual growth in your life and lasting peace in your heart.

1. *What comes to mind when you think of discipline? Explain.*

2. *How did your parents discipline you and your siblings when you were a child? How has that shaped the way you think about discipline as an adult?*

Experience

LEARN TO LIVE above your circumstances. This requires focused time with Me, the *One who overcame the world*. Trouble and distress are woven into the very fabric of this perishing world. Only My Life in you can empower you to face this endless flow of problems with *good cheer*.

As you sit quietly in My Presence, I shine Peace into your troubled mind and heart. Little by little, you are freed from earthly shackles and lifted up above your circumstances. You gain My perspective on your life, enabling you to distinguish between what is important and what is not. Rest in My Presence, *receiving Joy that no one can take away from you*.

– From *Jesus Calling*, March 13

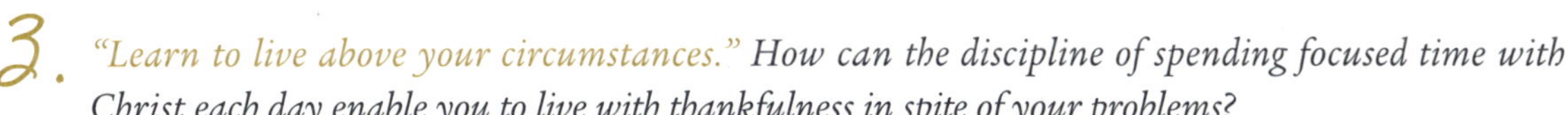

3. *"Learn to live above your circumstances." How can the discipline of spending focused time with Christ each day enable you to live with thankfulness in spite of your problems?*

4. *"Rest in My Presence." What tends to get in the way of you taking time each day to simply rest in Jesus' Presence? What helps you to remember to regularly set aside this time?*

Dwell

Read Hebrews 12:7–13. Like the best of fathers, God disciplines you, His beloved child, to train you in the way that you should go. Although this discipline may feel uncomfortable in the moment, it is an act of profound love on God's part that enables you to gain "[His] perspective on your life" and "distinguish between what is important and what is not." Said another way, it is God's discipline that allows you to grow in spiritual maturity so your mind can distinguish the things of God and "a harvest of righteousness" (verse 11) can be produced in your life.

5. *Trouble and distress "are woven into the very fabric of this perishing world." How does God often use such hardships in life for your benefit (see verse 7)?*

6. *Why is it important for you to willingly undergo God's discipline in your life?*

7. *Discipline produces "a harvest of righteousness and peace for those who have been trained by it" (verse 11). Does it surprise you to think of discipline this way? Explain your response.*

8. *The writer of Hebrews finishes by saying, "Strengthen your feeble arms and weak knees" (verse 12). What does this mean in terms of how you should view hardships in your life?*

Apply

The focus of this week's readings is on how God uses spiritual discipline to help you develop peace in your life of faith. Each day, read the passage slowly, pausing to think about what is being said. Remember, this is your opportunity to meet with Jesus every day of the week.

Day 1

Read Romans 5:3–5. *How difficult is it for you to "glory" in your sufferings? What makes the difference for a person who gains perseverance, character, and hope from suffering as opposed to someone who gives in to bitterness and despair?*

Day 2

Read 1 Peter 1:3–5. *Believers in Christ have a "living hope" (verse 3), which means confident expectation. What can you confidently expect because of the resurrection of Jesus Christ?*

Day 3

Read 1 Peter 1:6–9. *As a follower of Christ, you can greatly rejoice in your living hope and your eternal inheritance, even though for a little while you may have to suffer grief in trials. How does your confident hope for the future affect the way you face today's trials?*

Day 4

Read James 1:2–3. *James says that the testing of your faith produces perseverance. What is perseverance? Why is it valuable in the life of a follower of Christ?*

Day 5

Read James 1:4–5. *James encourages you to ask God for wisdom when dealing with trials. What is a current situation in which you need God's wisdom? How does this passage give you peace that God will answer your request when you ask for His wisdom?*

Day 6

Read Romans 8:16–18. *What reason for willingly sharing in Jesus' sufferings does Paul provide in verse 17? How do you respond to this? What reason for having peace in the midst of suffering does Paul provide in verse 18? How does this verse affect you?*

Day 7

Read Romans 8:22–25. *How real to you is the hope that Paul discusses? How much of this hope impacts you in the here and now when problems arise—and how much of this hope do you tend to regard as reserved for "way out in the future"? How can you strike a better balance?*

Week 49

JESUS AT THE CENTER

DISCOVER

From natural disasters, to health crises, to rising tensions across nations, the constant stream of disturbing news can leave us feeling unsettled. Add to that our personal worries, and it's no surprise that anxiety has become a daily struggle for so many people.

But here's the good news: God is in control even when life feels out of control. "In his hand are the depths of the earth" (Psalm 95:4). And the One who has the world in His hands invites you to have full faith in Him amid the uncertainty. When you put God first, focusing on His guidance and trusting in His love, He gives you peace that surpasses understanding.

In this week's study, you will turn to the words of Jesus and explore how His promises can help release your worries. Rest assured that with Jesus at the center of your life, you can face whatever lies ahead with courage and confidence!

1. *Do you tend to worry? If so, what are some recent things you've worried about? If not, how do you typically deal with challenges or uncertain situations?*

2. *Why do you think the tendency to worry is so prevalent among people today?*

Experience

You are on the path of My choosing. There is no randomness about your life. Here and Now comprise the coordinates of your daily life. Most people let their moments slip through their fingers, half-lived. They avoid the present by worrying about the future or longing for a better time and place. They forget that they are creatures who are subject to the limitations of time and space. They forget their Creator, who walks with them only in the present.

Every moment is alive with My glorious Presence, to those whose hearts are intimately connected with Mine. As you give yourself more and more to a life of constant communion with Me, you will find that you simply have no time for worry. Thus, you are freed to let My Spirit direct your steps, enabling you to walk along *the path of Peace*.

— From *Jesus Calling*, May 1

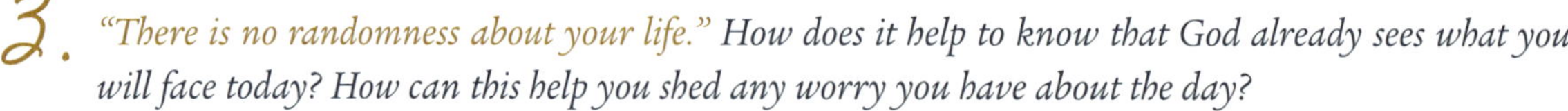

3. *"There is no randomness about your life." How does it help to know that God already sees what you will face today? How can this help you shed any worry you have about the day?*

4. *"Most people let their moments slip through their fingers, half-lived." Are you more likely to dwell on the past, worry about the future, or focus on the present? Explain your response.*

Dwell

Read Matthew 6:25–34. In this teaching, Jesus addresses the importance of allowing the Holy Spirit to "direct your steps, enabling you to walk along the path of Peace." He reminds you that if even the birds trust God to feed them, and the lilies trust Him to clothe them in beauty, you—His child—have nothing to worry about because you are far more valuable to Him. Jesus' timeless words encourage you to put your faith in God to provide what you truly need, according to His will. After all, your Father knows your every need and delights in helping you.

5. *It can be easy to forget that "there is no randomness about your life" and that God knows your every need—even before you do. What does Jesus say about this in verses 25–30?*

6. *What does Jesus say "the pagans" (those who do not serve the Lord) run after in this life? How should true followers of God—those who trust in Him—live differently?*

7. *What are some kingdom activities that demonstrate putting Jesus first, ahead of your worries about your own needs? (See, for example, Matthew 5:43–48 and 25:34–40.)*

8. *What would putting Jesus first, ahead of your worries, look like for you this week?*

Apply

The focus of this week's readings is on putting Jesus first in anxious times. Each day, read the passage slowly, pausing to think about what is being said and allowing it to sink into your heart. Remember, this is an opportunity to meet with Jesus and make Him the center of your life.

Day 1

Read Philippians 4:6–7. *How can you put the teachings of this passage into practice today?*

Day 2

Read Psalm 34:4. *How can you cultivate a greater sense of trust in God to overcome your fears?*

Day 3

Read Psalm 56:3. *How can understanding God's power and sovereignty help you overcome fear?*

Day 4

Read Psalm 63:1. *Do you thirst for Jesus, or do you mostly thirst for other things? Explain.*

Day 5

Read Psalm 63:2–5. *As a follower of Christ, in what ways have you beheld God's power and glory in your life?*

Day 6

Read Psalm 63:6–8. *What does it mean to keep God foremost in your thoughts "through the watches of the night" (verse 6)? Do you think this is meant to be taken literally? What would it take for you to make God that much of a priority?*

Day 7

Read Psalm 63:9–11. *When have you seen God triumph over an enemy's lies or threats in your life? What did that reveal to you about trusting Him?*

Week 50

FROM FEAR TO FAITH

Discover

King David faced many challenges and dangers during his life. He was hunted by King Saul. He was betrayed by his own son. He faced numerous military threats from Israel's hostile neighbors. A number of his psalms reflect these deep struggles he endured. In his prayers, he often cried out for protection and deliverance from his enemies.

Alhough your enemies might not be as obvious or as life-threatening, fear and anxiety can still take hold. Psalms like those of David repeatedly show you an inspiring path forward, urging you to focus on God rather than the threats you face. When fear rises, you should—like David—turn to God as your steadfast refuge, strength, and the One who brings lasting peace. When you shift from fear to faith, you find hope and comfort in Jesus' presence.

In this week's study the goal is for you to start work on adopting a faith-filled mindset, knowing that God is greater than anything you fear.

1. *What are some threats in the world today? How do those threats impact your life?*

2. *What do you do when you encounter a situation that causes you fear? How do you tend to handle the stress you feel?*

Experience

I WANT TO BE CENTRAL in your entire being. When your focus is firmly on Me, My Peace displaces fears and worries. They will encircle you, seeking entrance, so you must stay alert. Let trust and thankfulness stand guard, turning back fear before it can gain a foothold. *There is no fear in My Love,* which shines on you continually. Sit quietly in My Love-Light while I bless you with radiant Peace. Turn your whole being to trusting and loving Me.

— From *Jesus Calling*, June 3

3. *"My Peace displaces fears and worries." When have your fears tried to intrude on the Peace that Jesus has given you as one of His own? What did you do in response?*

4. *"There is no fear in My Love." Have you ever considered that Jesus' Love should leave no room for fear in your life? What would it look like to truly live without fear?*

DWELL

Read Psalm 71:1–24. The writer of this psalm (likely David) understood that "[God's] Peace displaces fears and worries." What starts as a heartfelt request for rescue quickly turns into a bold declaration of trust—as if God's deliverance is already assured. This deep faith in God is clearly something the psalmist had relied on throughout his life. His example reminds us that we too can trust in God for help in our most challenging circumstances.

5. *The psalmist begins by stating, "In you, LORD, I have taken refuge" (verse 1). What does this reveal about his current situation? What was he professing in this opening verse?*

6. *The psalmist speaks of hope in verses 5 and 14. Biblical hope is not wishful thinking but an expectation that what God promised will come to pass. How does keeping "your focus firmly on [Christ]" and remembering His past works enable you to have this kind of hope?*

7. *The psalmist states several times in verses 15–18 that he will proclaim God's mighty deeds. Why is it important to remember God's acts in the past when you are facing times of fear?*

8. *Picture the psalmist sitting "quietly in [God's] Love-Light" as he wrote out these verses. How would you describe his level of peace by the end of the psalm?*

Apply

The focus of this week's readings is on how you can turn to Jesus in the midst of your fears. Each day, read the passage slowly, pausing to reflect on what is being said. Remember, this is an opportunity to meet with Jesus and look to Him as the stronghold of your life.

Day 1

Read Psalm 27:1–3. *For a Christian, what does it mean to say that the Lord is your light? What does it mean to say that the Lord is your stronghold?*

Day 2

Read Psalm 27:4–6. *What confidence does the psalmist express in God's deliverance from his trials? What would it look like for you to have this same confidence in all your trials?*

Day 3

Read Psalm 27:7–9. *As a Christian, do you believe Jesus hears your voice when you call? What helps you to believe this? What gets in the way?*

Day 4

Read Psalm 27:10. *Have your father or mother let you down? How have you seen the Lord through the filter of your parents? How is He a better parent?*

Day 5

Read Psalm 27:11–12. *Who are the "false witnesses" (verse 12) that rise up against you? What can you be confident about them if Jesus is truly number one in your life?*

Day 6

Read Psalm 27:13. *How confident are you that you will see "the goodness of the* Lord *in the land of the living"? Why? Why should you have that confidence if you're a believer in Christ?*

Day 7

Read Psalm 27:14. *What does it mean to "wait for the* Lord*" in your current season of life? Why does it take courage to wait for Him?*

Week 51

SEARCHING FOR WISDOM

Discover

It's natural to think about God's guidance in terms of life's big-picture questions—"Which career should I choose?" "Who should I marry?" "Should we have children or just get a dog?" Yet the Bible calls you to an even greater quest: to continually seek God not only in the major decisions but also in the daily, ordinary moments.

Knowing God's will is about more than getting answers. Above all, it's about seeking His presence and wisdom. It's about committing "whatever you do" to the Lord and believing that "he will establish your plans" (Proverbs 16:3). Day by day, moment by moment, God invites you to trust Him in the small things, building a foundation of faith for uncertain times.

In this week's study you will explore what God says about daily turning to Him for direction—in both the big things and small things. When you seek Him first, He will light your way through the unknown and lead you toward His greater plan, one step at a time.

1. *When you're seeking to discern God's will or are in need of wisdom, is your main focus usually on God's answers or His Presence? Explain your response.*

2. *What are a few of the smaller decisions that God has used to build your foundation of faith in His wisdom? List a few in the space below.*

Experience

I AM YOUR LORD! Seek Me as Friend and Lover of your soul, but remember that I am also King of kings—sovereign over all. You can make some plans as you gaze into the day that stretches out before you. But you need to hold those plans tentatively, anticipating that I may have other ideas. The most important thing to determine is what to do right now. Instead of scanning the horizon of your life, looking for things that need to be done, concentrate on the task before you and the One who never leaves your side. Let everything else fade into the background. This will unclutter your mind, allowing Me to occupy more and more of your consciousness.

Trust Me to show you what to do when you have finished what you are doing now. I will guide you step by step as you bend your will to Mine. Thus you stay close to Me on the *path of Peace.*

— From *Jesus Calling*, May 16

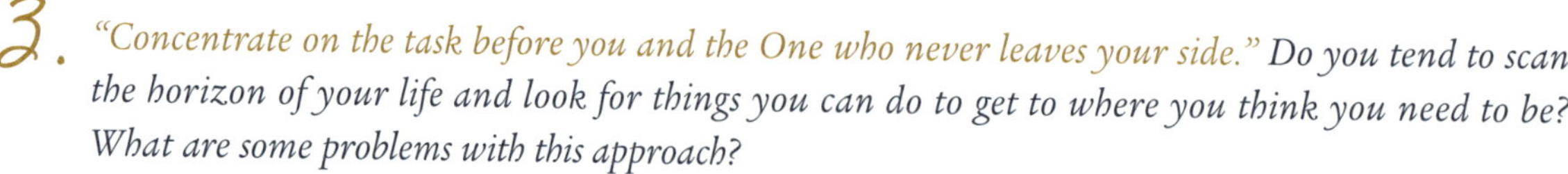

3. *"Concentrate on the task before you and the One who never leaves your side." Do you tend to scan the horizon of your life and look for things you can do to get to where you think you need to be? What are some problems with this approach?*

4. *"Trust Me to show you what to do when you have finished what you are doing now." How easy or difficult is it for you to trust Jesus with the next step instead of planning everything out in detail? Why do you think God often reveals His plan one step at a time?*

DWELL

Read Job 28:12–28. Job exemplified unwavering integrity in the face of immense trials. Despite losing his children, his wealth, and his health, and enduring accusations from friends who believed he was being punished for hidden sins, this godly man stood firm in his faith and commitment to righteousness. In this chapter, Job reflects on wisdom as the divinely given ability to think and act rightly amid life's challenges. It emphasizes that true wisdom comes from God and you can trust Him to "guide you step by step as you bend your will to [His]."

5. *Job states that wisdom cannot "be bought" through any human means (see verses 14–19). What does this reveal about the source of wisdom? What does it reveal about its value?*

6. *Job ultimately concludes that only God "understands the way" to wisdom (verse 23). What should your first course of action thus be when you need direction in life?*

7. *Job states that "the fear of the LORD—that is wisdom" (verse 28). How does the fear of the Lord (your reverence, respect, and awe of God) affect the way you think about acquiring wisdom and discerning His will when you don't have a clear answer?*

8. *You will make "plans as you gaze into the day that stretches out before you." How will you seek God's wisdom today as you make those plans and submit them to His will?*

Apply

The focus of this week's readings is on seeking God's wisdom during times of uncertainty. Each day, read the passage slowly, pausing to think about what is being said. Remember, this is an opportunity to meet with Jesus and actively seek the wisdom that only He can provide.

Day 1

Read 1 Kings 3:5–10. *What did Solomon recognize about the importance of having wisdom? Why do you think the Lord was pleased with Solomon's request?*

Day 2

Read Proverbs 19:21. *When have you seen the truth of this proverb play out in your life? How did that experience affect your intimacy with Jesus during your uncertain times?*

Day 3

Read Psalm 34:8–10. *What is the promise for those who fear the Lord? What will you receive when you honestly "seek the Lord" (verse 10)?*

Day 4

Read Psalm 34:11–14. *How does the concept of fearing the Lord personally influence your decisions and actions throughout the day?*

Day 5

Read Proverbs 2:1–2. *What should your attitude be when it comes to seeking God's wisdom? What are some practical ways to store up God's commands?*

Day 6

Read Proverbs 2:3–5. *How do you go about searching for wisdom as hidden treasure? Why is it important to develop a habit of seeking God's wisdom in this way?*

Day 7

Read Proverbs 2:6–8. *When the writer says the Lord "holds success in store for the upright" (verse 7), he doesn't mean that those who lead godly lives will be successful in all their efforts. Rather, he means the upright are generally more likely to succeed in life. Does this motivate you to lead a godly life? Or do you want a more ironclad guarantee? Explain your response.*

Week 52

IN THE PROPER PLACE

DISCOVER

During this study, we have explored the importance of sitting in God's presence, placing our trust and hope in God, finding joy, courage, and wisdom in difficult times, and being grateful to a God who is always loving. God calls us to put Him above everything else and trust Him as the only one who can truly fulfill our physical and spiritual needs. When we prioritize other things, we end up serving them as if they were gods.

This struggle is not new to just us. In the Bible, the Israelites faced the same problem. Despite God's command to have no other gods before Him (see Exodus 20:3), they repeatedly turned to idols. While we might not worship statues of wood or stone today, we still are tempted to turn to things other than God to meet our needs. An idol is anything we love more than Jesus or prioritize above Him.

Jesus calls us to remove these idols and make Him our First Love. In this final session, we will consider the allure of idols, identify some things we are tempted to idolize, and discover how we can turn to biblical truths to overcome them.

1. *What are some pursuits that people in the world put ahead of Jesus today?*

2. *Why do you think people so often devote themselves to such idols?*

Experience

WORSHIP ME ONLY. Whatever occupies your mind the most becomes your god. Worries, if indulged, develop into idols. Anxiety gains a life of its own, parasitically infesting your mind. Break free from this bondage by affirming your trust in Me and refreshing yourself in My Presence. What goes on in your mind is invisible, undetectable to other people. But I read your thoughts continually, searching for evidence of trust in Me. I rejoice when your mind turns toward Me. Guard your thoughts diligently; good thought-choices will keep you close to Me.

– From *Jesus Calling*, January 30

3. *"Anxiety gains a life of its own, parasitically infesting your mind." What types of worries "infest" your mind the most? Has this been the case for a long time or has this thing dominated your thoughts only for a season?*

4. *"Break free from this bondage." How should you shake off the bondage of an idol? Have you ever successfully done this? If so, how did doing it affect you?*

Dwell

Read Isaiah 30:19–26 and consider the statement, "Whatever occupies your mind the most becomes your god." Isaiah had previously warned the Israelites that the Assyrians would attack because they had turned to idols instead of seeking God. But now the prophet changes his focus and foretells what will happen when the people decide to trust in God and change their ways. As you read, note that *Zion* refers to Jerusalem, Israel's capital city.

5. *What promise did God give to the people of Jerusalem if they cried out to Him for help? What would be "hidden no more" from them (verse 20)?*

6. *What assurance of direction did God say He would provide to His people (see verse 21)? Why did they especially need this guidance at this point (see verse 22)?*

7. *What blessings would the redeemed receive when they cast away their idols (see verses 23–24)? What blessings have you received in your life when you cast away your idols?*

8. *What does God say about the way He would heal His people (see verse 26)? How do all these promises of hope, healing, restoration, and blessing encourage you today?*

Apply

The focus of this final reading is putting your faith in God and not trusting in idols. Each day, read the passage slowly, pausing to think about what is being said. Remember, this is an opportunity to meet with Jesus and determine to put Him first in your life.

Day 1

Read Exodus 32:1–3. *These events took place just after the Lord had freed the Israelites from slavery in Egypt, rescued them from the Egyptians, and led them to Mount Sinai for further instructions. Given all God had done, why did the people so easily forget His care for them?*

Day 2

Read Exodus 32:4–6. *Why do you think Aaron and the people chose to turn back to idolatry at this time? What is so appealing about the gods our culture turns to in times of distress?*

Day 3

Read Exodus 32:7–11. *How did the Lord respond when the people had a party to celebrate their new idol? Why do you think the Lord responded in this way?*

Day 4

Read Exodus 32:12–14. *How did Moses persuade the Lord not to destroy His people? What does Moses' approach tell you about the God you serve?*

Day 5

Read Exodus 32:25–35. *The people were "running wild" and "out of control" (verse 25). How did Moses address this problem of idolatry? How did the Lord address it?*

Day 6

Read Deuteronomy 7:1–6. *How does the Lord want you to relate to a person who has been spiritually led astray by another individual?*

Day 7

Read Deuteronomy 7:7–11. *What motivations does this passage give you for obeying the Lord?*

ABOUT SARAH YOUNG

Sarah Young, author of the bestselling 365-day devotionals *Jesus Calling®* and *Jesus Listens*, was committed to helping people connect with Jesus and the Bible. Her books have sold more than 46 million copies worldwide. *Jesus Calling®* has appeared on all major bestseller lists. Sarah's writings include *Jesus Calling®*, *Jesus Listens®*, *Jesus Always*, *Jesus Today®*, *Jesus Lives™*, *Dear Jesus*, *Jesus Calling® for Little Ones*, *Jesus Calling® Bible Storybook*, *Jesus Calling®: 365 Devotions for Kids*, and more, each encouraging readers in their journeys toward intimacy with Christ. Sarah believed praying for her readers was a privilege and God-given responsibility and did so daily even amidst her own health challenges.

Connect with Jesus Calling at:

Facebook.com/JesusCalling
Instagram.com/JesusCalling
Youtube.com/JesusCallingBook
Pinterest.com/Jesus_Calling

From the Publisher

GREAT STUDIES

ARE EVEN BETTER WHEN THEY'RE SHARED!

Help others find this study:

- Post a review at your favorite online bookseller.
- Post a picture on a social media account and share why you enjoyed it.
- Send a note to a friend who would also love it—or, better yet, go through it with them!

Thanks for helping others grow their faith!